TEACHING SHAKESF
IN PRIMARY SCHOOL

Teaching Shakespeare in Primary Schools offers guidance and practical ideas for teaching Shakespeare's plays across Key Stage 1 and 2. It demonstrates how the plays can engage young readers in exciting, immersive and fun literacy lessons and illustrates how Shakespeare's powerful themes, iconic characters and rich language remain relevant today.

Part 1 explores the place of classic texts in modern classrooms – how teachers can invite children to make meaning from Shakespeare's words – and considers key issues such as gender and race, and embraces modern technology and digital storytelling. Part 2 presents Shakespeare's plays: *The Tempest, A Midsummer Night's Dream, Romeo and Juliet, Julius Caesar, Macbeth* and *The Winter's Tale*. For each play, there is a suggested sequence of activities that will guide teachers through the process of inspiring children, incubating ideas and making connections all before responding to it through drama, writing and other subjects.

You don't need to be an actor, a scholar or even an extrovert to get the best out of Shakespeare! Written by experienced teachers, this book is an essential resource for teachers of all levels of experience who want to teach creative, engaging and memorable lessons.

Stefan Kucharczyk is the founder of ARTiculate Education, an independent creative consultancy for schools. He is an experienced primary school teacher, and his research interests include creativity in education, digital literacy, Star Wars in the classroom and filmmaking. He is an associate lecturer at the Open University.

Maureen Kucharczyk is a highly experienced primary school teacher from Wolverhampton. Over three decades as senior teacher and literacy leader, she has specialised in creative approaches to children's literacy and writing. Her teaching interests include engaging boys with writing, Shakespeare, drama and poetry.

"This engaging and accessible text will bring Shakespeare's plays to life for teachers and children across the next decade. Rich, varied and highly stimulating, *Teaching Shakespeare in Primary Schools: All the World's a Stage* is packed with practical advice and structured ways to explore the work of the bard in their classrooms. The energy, tone and creativity evident in the Kucharczyks' text will support both experienced and less assured primary practitioners."

Professor Teresa Cremin, *The Open University, UK*

"This is not simply a book about Shakespeare but one that sponsors a love and lustre for those who wish to promote a love of learning and language. The text looks at the relevance of word play and linguistic analysis, providing practical and accessible examples of how to develop a passion for literature and ignite the imagination of children when introducing them to a range of Shakespeare's plays. Packed with ideas for teaching, we see how to expertly deconstruct, reassemble, infer meaning from, identify key themes within and deliver language with passion, purpose and gusto!

The relevance of the works for a 21st-century audience is examined in an accessible and entertaining format. This book is engaging from the off, inviting the reader to re-evaluate their previous experiences of Shakespeare, always through our authors' expert reimagined eye."

Megan Stephenson, *Leeds Trinity University, UK*

TEACHING SHAKESPEARE IN PRIMARY SCHOOLS

All the World's a Stage

Stefan Kucharczyk and Maureen Kucharczyk

Routledge
Taylor & Francis Group

LONDON AND NEW YORK

First published 2022
by Routledge
2 Park Square, Milton Park, Abingdon, Oxon OX14 4RN

and by Routledge
605 Third Avenue, New York, NY 10158

Routledge is an imprint of the Taylor & Francis Group, an informa business

© 2022 Stefan Kucharczyk and Maureen Kucharczyk

British Library Cataloguing-in-Publication Data
A catalogue record for this book is available from the British Library

Library of Congress Cataloging-in-Publication Data
Names: Kucharczyk, Stefan, author. | Kucharczyk, Maureen, author.
Title: Teaching Shakespeare in primary schools : all the world's a stage /
    Stefan Kucharczyk and Maureen Kucharczyk.
Description: Abingdon, Oxon ; New York : Routledge, 2022. | Includes bibliographical
    references and index.
Identifiers: LCCN 2021013962 | ISBN 9780367903503 (hardback) |
    ISBN 9780367903510 (paperback) | ISBN 9781003023944 (ebook)
Subjects: LCSH: Shakespeare, William, 1564-1616–Study and teaching (Primary) |
    LCGFT: Instructional and educational works.
Classification: LCC PR2987 .K83 2022 | DDC 822.3/3–dc23
LC record available at https://lccn.loc.gov/2021013962

ISBN: 978-0-367-90350-3 (hbk)
ISBN: 978-0-367-90351-0 (pbk)
ISBN: 978-1-003-02394-4 (ebk)

DOI: 10.4324/9781003023944

Typeset in Interstate
by Apex CoVantage, LLC

All the world's a stage,
And all the men and women merely players;
They have their exits and their entrances,
And one *human* in *their* time plays many parts,

William Shakespeare, updated.
As You Like It (Act II, Scene 7)

CONTENTS

ACKNOWLEDGEMENTS

For both authors, this book has been a labour of love. We have many people to thank for ensuring love's labours were not lost. Please accept our apologies for that terrible pun. In particular, we would like to thank Megan Stephenson (Leeds Trinity University) and Professor Jonathan Glazzard (Edge Hill University) for their astute feedback and words of encouragement. This was much appreciated. Similarly, we would like to thank Ed Podesta (Leeds Trinity University) for dusting off his Hamlet doublet to share insightful suggestions on the book as well as his experience of treading the boards.

We would also like to thank the following teachers for their recommendations, expertise and time. They are Katja Rudden, Jennifer Williamson and Tom Neal. Many thanks.

Introduction

Encountering Shakespeare

William Shakespeare was born in Stratford-upon-Avon in 1564. Fifty-two years later, on 23 April 1616 – supposedly also his birthdate – he died. Between his first breath and his last, William Shakespeare found time to author 37 plays (solo and in collaboration), 154 sonnets and several other poems, as well as sign a few contracts and property deeds. In 1623, his collection of plays, often called the *First Folio*, was published in London. In his lifetime, his writing established his name and fortune on the stages of London's playhouses, notably the Globe Theatre. He married Anne Hathaway in 1582, fathered two daughters, Susanna and Judith, and a son, Hamnet, who passed away in childhood.

OK, that's enough of that. Such is the status attached to the word 'Shakespeare' that it is easy to feel daunted, or rather distracted by the spectre of the man – like Banquo haunting the feast in *Macbeth* – when approaching his plays to read, watch or teach. Yet almost all that is known with any certainty about his life is contained in the first paragraph of this book. Moreover, it probably doesn't matter. That is not to dismiss or reduce him in any way, just to say that understanding Shakespeare's life adds little to how we read his plays, so it is good to get it out of the way early.

In the centuries after his death, Shakespeare remained known in London, England, and later around the world as England's most famous author. The biography of his life has been a reliable source of scholarly writing ever since. The countless thousands of pages written try in various ways to uncover the genius of Shakespeare: the man known as the Bard, the immortal Bard, the Bard of Avon, the Sweet Swan of Avon and – if you're not a fan – the 'upstart crow'. The British Library catalogue, for example, holds at least 9000 books listed as Shakespeare biographies. If you don't have time to read *all* of those, Stephen Greenblatt's *Will in the World* (2016) and Bill Bryson's *Shakespeare* (2007) are all highly readable modern introductions. *Shakespeare: An Oxford Guide* (Wells and Orlin, 2003) is one of many comprehensive scholarly explorations of Shakespeare and his times.

We didn't want to write a book about William Shakespeare. As we have shown, there are already plenty of those. Instead, we wanted to write something more personal about how we, two primary school teachers from Shakespeare's neck of the woods, rediscovered a love of Shakespeare's work by teaching it. In doing so, we began to see Shakespeare not as a lofty cultural monolith, but as a voice that can still speak to us and the children we teach in the 21st century. That voice is not a booming theatrical Brian Blessed monologue, but simply

DOI: 10.4324/9781003023944-1

one side of an ongoing dialogue. And like any worthwhile conversation, it needs two voices: Shakespeare's voice and ours – both questioning, both answering, both learning and understanding. It is a conversation that deepens with time, and as we have found, one that finds new meaning through the eyes, ears and mouths of children.

Live long and Prosper(o)

Researchers have pored over the meaning, reading, performance and inspiration behind Shakespeare's works for many centuries, and this continues to this day. Such research extends far beyond those interested in literature or the dramatic arts. The food in Shakespeare's plays (Fitzpatrick, 2013), Shakespeare's dramatic animals (Shannon, 2009) and 'a Buddhist Shakespeare' (Howe, 1994) are just some, decidedly niche, examples of research into Shakespeare's works. His plays have been translated into most Earthly languages as well as the *Star Trek* language Klingon (Kazimierczak, 2010), DNA code (Ewing Duncan, 2013) and even a wearable watch that bleeps Shakespeare's sonnets in Morse Code.

First encounters with Shakespeare

Even though the authors of this book attended school three decades apart, there are parallels between our first encounters with Shakespeare – Maureen in the 1960s, Stefan in the 1990s. These parallels are perhaps both at once surprising and not so surprising. Firstly, we both studied Shakespeare for the first time at secondary school. Shakespeare was still regarded then as a rite of passage, suitable for older readers only who had reached an intellectual threshold to begin to 'get' Shakespeare. Secondly, the first play we encountered was *Julius Caesar*, taught faithfully in the original language. Thirdly, we read it in precisely the same way: Banda-copied scripts, dog-eared and filled with last year's annotations, were distributed around the class. Parts were assigned and, taking turns from our seats, we read from page one as Shakespeare's portrait, snipped from a magazine, gazed from the wall like literary royalty. Needless to say, it was the experience, rather than the content, that left the greater impression. The language was dense and hard to pronounce. Maureen, asked to take a turn reading a key line, recalls the embarrassment of delivering "Et tu, Brute?" with the English, or rather West Midlands pronunciation – "Et tu, Broot?". Cue athletic eye-rolls and a chorus of sniggers from the around the class. "It's Bru-*tay*," corrected the exasperated teacher.

If it was hard to say, it was even harder to imagine. Gazing out of the window at a wet playing-field on a grey Wolverhampton morning (admittedly this detail is unprovable, but statistically likely), it was hard to conjure the majesty and intrigues of ancient Rome while we sat at our desks. Note the word 'sat'. Even half of Shakespeare's audiences at the Globe Theatre would have stood, but we remained seated, waiting our turn to speak. True, it was thrilling when Caesar got stabbed in the Senate; but with nothing to actually *see* and only the stage directions to go by (and no chance to practise on each other with rulers) it was all a bit underwhelming.

Perhaps you were luckier. Perhaps Shakespeare was brought to life by a passionate parent or teacher, and you were encouraged to speak, move and feel as you read his words aloud. As we will explain in later chapters of this book, Shakespeare lives in moving, mixing and making: making noise, decisions and choices. British poet James Anthony said that he didn't get Shakespeare at first, but his inspirational teacher left a "smouldering curiosity", one that later led him to write a collection of Shakespeare's sonnets in contemporary English (Anthony, 2018). Sadly, it is just as likely that your first encounters with the Sweet Swan of Avon were similar to ours. More like a dead duck. It left us wondering whether Shakespeare really had anything to say to people like us, in our time, in Wolverhampton, or what the fuss was about.

Those who work in education today might imagine that pedagogy would have moved on between the 1960s and 1990s. As society became more pluralist, less reverent, it might have been expected there would be less slavish attention to the intricacies of early modern English and more attention given to what we thought about it. Unsurprising, because it hadn't. A further 30 years later, as heritage literature – the 'classics' – makes a return to English primary classrooms, and grammar drills become the focal point for understanding language at the expense of drama and creativity, it could be said that things still haven't evolved far enough.

For both of us, teachers later in our education introduced us to drama and elements of aesthetics and performance (Stefan recalls even being allowed *to stand up* to deliver a line in part of *The Tempest*). Little by little, the brilliance of Shakespeare's works became more evident. We began to see how the characters stood for something larger, and how beautiful and powerful it could be to speak the words out loud, even if we didn't understand all of what it meant.

As adults, we both worked as primary school teachers with a passion for English. Inspired by Shakespeare's cultural significance, his ubiquity and maybe a little of the God-like awe we had encountered at school, we felt this was something important that we needed to share with our classes. But influenced by our experiences at school, we felt we had to make the plays 'live' – in both pronunciations of the word – and to show children how the plots, themes and characters can resonate with their lives. Maybe Julius Caesar reminds us of a bossy child taking over our games; the Capulets and Montagues remind us of rival playground cliques; the unrequited love of Hermia for Lysander in *A Midsummer Night's Dream* could easily be the girl we fancied, but who had eyes only for someone else.

No, we're not Shakespeare scholars, and nor do we have a background in the performing arts. Instead, we are primary school teachers, book lovers and Bardolators (this is a real word . . .) who have felt our way along by instinct, intuition and a love of literature. Maybe by following our path, you will be the teacher who sparks a child's smouldering curiosity about Shakespeare, ready to fully ignite it when they meet him again later in their education.

"'Tis the times' plague": Covid 19 and the performing arts

At the time of writing, in 2021, the world was recovering from the restrictions and damage wrought by the coronavirus pandemic. As places of performance – schools, theatres, cinemas, galleries, sports stadia – closed around the world, the economic and emotional impact on those who work in the performing arts has been severe. But as we stayed indoors, cut off from our families, friends and fellow citizens, it brought into sharper relief how enriching live performance is to our existence. Like King Leontes in *The Winter's Tale* realising his love for his daughter and wife only once they are banished, the authors of this book – along with millions of others around the world – mourned the loss of live performances even more strongly when we found them suddenly absent. Subscription television, movies on demand and online streaming are all well and good, but they cannot ever match the atmosphere of a living, breathing, for-one-night-only performance. Introducing these unique experiences to children is more than just part of an education: it is an essential component of a culturally rich life.

The origins of this book

The idea for this book began in 2014 following the implementation of the overhauled National Curriculum in England which encouraged primary school teachers to use heritage literature as a core part of their primary literacy teaching. We met teachers at varying career stages as well as graduate students who wanted (or who were required) to teach Shakespeare to their primary pupils but did not know where to begin. In many cases, they had experienced Shakespeare as we had and were dreading the thought of the complex language, the bored faces and the struggle to get children to produce assessable writing from it.

This book aims to add to the growing collection of books promoting active, creative, social and inclusive teaching of Shakespeare's plays. *Teaching Shakespeare* by Rex Gibson (1998) is credited with reimagining the teaching and learning of Shakespeare's plays as a collaborative experience. While we endorse this approach and have drawn on his work in our own teaching and in the writing of this book, Gibson's approach largely focuses on secondary education and so is less useful for teachers of primary school literacy.

The RSC Shakespeare Toolkit for Primary Teachers by the Royal Shakespeare Company (2014) offers a valuable collection of resources for primary school teachers. Yet it focuses on only three highly popular plays – *Macbeth*, *A Midsummer Night's Dream* and *Romeo and Juliet* – mostly with upper Key Stage 2 in mind. For teachers in Key Stage 1 or for experienced teachers looking for variety or a new challenge, this text might also seem limited.

There are many other books available to teachers, yet many felt rooted in the 20th (or 19th) century: they lack practical guidance on how to meet the demands of 21st-century education or how to satisfy the interests of children who enjoy exploring stories using filmmaking, animation or other forms of interactive and digital storytelling. Resources based around worksheets may be useful to a busy schoolteacher, but rendered studying Shakespeare a desk-bound, passive experience.

Above all, we felt that many of these books make one shaky assumption: that the reader recognises that teaching Shakespeare to young children is a good idea. From experience, we know that often, many feel the opposite is true. While teachers may have respect for Shakespeare's fame and legacy, it is the same wary respect you may have for a leopard: you can appreciate its beauty, its power and the ingenuity of its design, but you wouldn't feel confident taking it for a walk, and you certainly don't want it in your house or near young children.

This book presents an approach to teaching Shakespeare that can satisfy what children need as socially, emotionally and technologically savvy learners, and support teachers to teach through, across and beyond the limitations of the National Curriculum. In doing so, we argue that Shakespeare's plays were intended to be *performed*, not just read. In doing so in the 21st century, teachers need to embrace digital technology for telling stories along-side traditional approaches to creative writing. Above all, we want teachers to present these plays, not as a relic from another age, but as a direct link to an inherited history, culture and lineage of stories for all to read, enjoy and understand.

Who is this book for?

This book was written with many intended readers in mind. While in line with the objectives of the English National Curriculum (DfE, 2013), we are aware that Shakespeare's universal appeal means his plays are studied in classrooms across the UK and around the world. As such, we have taken care to ensure that the activities can easily be adapted by teachers to meet the aims of other curricula.

For **primary school teachers** of all levels of experience in both Key Stage 1 and 2, this book offers practical advice from experienced practitioners on how to bring Shakespeare into the classroom. We offer much-needed advice on how to present Shakespeare to younger readers (especially in Key Stage 1, where available materials are very limited), how to manage drama lessons and how to teach Shakespeare in a holistic way through the core areas of the literacy curriculum and as part of a cross-curricular project.

Newly and recently qualified teachers (NQT/RQT) will find practical advice on how to teach six Shakespeare plays and the basics of drama, critical reading and creative writing. **Experienced teachers** or those who have taught Shakespeare before will find a range of fresh and interesting ideas – such as digital storytelling and film – to inspire children to read, perform and create from Shakespeare's plays.

Equally, for **pre-service teachers** or **undergraduate students**, this book offers guidance on the key pedagogical approaches suitable for exploring the plays of Shakespeare. The rationale for using heritage literature (Chapter 1) and the themes, issues and opportunities of 21st-century teaching and learning (Chapter 2) will frame an approach to teaching literature that we have found effective.

For **literacy and English subject coordinators**, this book offers the rationale for intro-ducing Shakespeare to your school's literacy curriculum and lays the foundation for a whole-school approach to literacy. The practical activities highlighted in Part 2 will be useful as a guide to teachers on where to start. The chapters in Part 1 have been written to equip you with the answers to help encourage and support staff who may need convincing of why this is a good idea in the first place!

For **drama specialists** or **drama group leaders**, this book may offer new activities to try with children and offer direction on how to enable schools to embed Shakespeare, drama and performance as part of the wider curriculum.

How to use this book

This book is written in two parts. Part 1 deals with the context and rationale for teaching Shakespeare in 21st-century primary schools. Part 2 offers a guide to teaching six of Shakespeare's plays to both Key Stage 1 and Key Stage 2.

Part 1

Chapter 1 starts with the question 'Why teach Shakespeare in primary schools?'. We explore the educational and developmental impact of teaching Shakespeare's plays and address some of the debates around the place of heritage literature in 21st-century schools.

Chapter 2 takes this idea further and explores how Shakespeare can be relevant to social issues and learning preferences of 21st-century children. We highlight key approaches that underlie child-centred teaching of Shakespeare, especially what Emma Smith calls Shakespeare's 'permissive gappiness' and how teachers can show Shakespeare's work through the lens of children's lived experiences.

Chapter 3 is written in two parts or *acts* (no eye-rolls please – this is Shakespeare after all!) **Act I** deals with 'words' and considers language, texts and reading Shakespeare's plays. **Act II** deals with 'deeds' and examines approaches for responding to Shakespeare's plays through drama and creative writing.

Part 2

In Part 2, we move to the schemes of work for developing a whole-school approach to teaching Shakespeare in primary literacy. **Chapters 4 to 9** each look at one of Shakespeare's most famous plays, which have been carefully chosen to suit the primary year groups, Year 1 to Year 6: *The Tempest*, *A Midsummer Night's Dream*, *Romeo and Juliet*, *Julius Caesar*, *Macbeth* and *The Winter's Tale*.

The activities we provide by no means represent a comprehensive, exhaustive or prescriptive scheme of work. Indeed, it is the opposite. Every school has different children, teachers and priorities, and, although these activities are designed in line with the English National Curriculum (2013), we have left them intentionally loose so they could equally be taught in classrooms in Scotland, Sweden, Sudan or Singapore. They are flexible to allow your teaching to be responsive to the children you know, which is an approach we strongly encourage. As a teacher, you will know best how to fit these activities into your planning depending on how much time and flexibility you have.

The teaching materials

To support a whole-school approach, the guidance for teaching each play is structured in a similar way.

1 **Background to the play:** This section offers an overview of key ideas in the play, a summary of the plot, the historical context for the play and chosen key quotations.
2 **Teaching the play:** In this section, we explain how to structure a series of lessons on each play. The teaching sequence is structured as follows:

Inspiration
- How the play will be revealed to the children in an imaginative and captivating way.

Incubation
- Discussing ideas, themes and characters in the play.
- Embedding key vocabulary.

Connection
- Ways in which the play can be linked to other areas of the National Curriculum to form a cross-curricular unit of work.

Illustration
- Ideas for how you can bring the story to life through art.

Application
- Guidance on how to develop children's creative ideas into writing, digital texts and performances.

In each chapter, we also:

- Show how the plays can be explored through digital technology.
- Offer general advice for how the plays might be made inclusive for learners with SEND and for multilingual learners.
- Detail how these activities meet the objectives for the English National Curriculum (2013) (see Appendix 1).

3 **Resources:** In each chapter, we offer a list of recommended print and digital versions of the story and additional resources to support your teaching.

Reading

Recommended reading

Bryson, B. (2007) *Eminent Lives: Shakespeare*, London: Harper Press.
Greenblatt, S. (2016) *Will in the World: How Shakespeare Became Shakespeare*, London: The Bodley Head.

Online resources

www.rsc.org.uk/education/ The website of the Royal Shakespeare Company contains resources for teachers and information about Shakespeare and his plays.

www.shakespearesglobe.com/discover/ **The Globe Theatre** in London offer free audio and video resources to support teaching Shakespeare, including excellent wordless animations of key plays and a virtual tour of the theatre.

References

Anthony, J. (2018) *Shakespeare's Sonnets, Retold*, London: Penguin.

Department for Education (2013) *The National Curriculum in England: Key Stages 1 and 2 Framework Document* Available at: www.gov.uk/government/publications/national-curriculum-in-england-primary-curriculum [Accessed 1 January 2021].

Ewing Duncan, D. (2013) 'Translating Shakespeare into DNA Code,' *The Atlantic* [ONLINE] Available at: www.theatlantic.com/health/archive/2013/02/translating-shakespeare-into-dna/273287/ [Accessed 1 December 2020].

Fitzpatrick, J. (2013) *Food in Shakespeare: Early Modern Dietaries and the Plays*, Aldershot: Ashgate Publishing.

Gibson, R. (1998) *Teaching Shakespeare*, Cambridge: Cambridge University Press.

Howe, J. (1994) *A Buddhist's Shakespeare: Affirming Self-Deconstructions*, Vancouver: Fairleigh Dickinson University Press.

Kazimierczak, K. (2010) 'Adapting Shakespeare for "Star Trek" and "Star Trek" for Shakespeare: "The Klingon Hamlet" and the Spaces of Translation,' *Studies in Popular Culture*, Volume 32, Issue 2 (Spring 2010), pp. 35-55.

Royal Shakespeare Company (RSC) (2014) *The RSC Shakespeare Toolkit for Primary Teachers*, London: Methuen Drama.

Shannon, L. (2009) 'The Eight Animals in Shakespeare: Or, before the Human,' *PMLA*, Volume 124, Isuue 2 (March), pp. 472-479.

Wells, S. and Orlin, L. C. (Eds.) (2003) *Shakespeare: An Oxford Guide*, Oxford: Oxford University Press.

Part 1 Shakespeare and 21st-century education

1   Why teach Shakespeare?

In a sketch from a 1999 TV special of the historical comedy *Blackadder*, time-travelling butler Edmund Blackadder accidently collides with a man carrying a sheaf of papers. As the man falls to the ground, Blackadder realises that this is none other than William Shakespeare. Blackadder then does two things. He asks for his signature, then punches him in the mouth. "That's for every schoolboy and schoolgirl for the next four hundred years!" he says. "Have you any idea of the suffering you're going to cause!" (Blackadder: Back & Forth, 1999)

This moment captures perfectly the relationship we have with Shakespeare today. His face, as captured in the Droeshout engraving, is instantly recognisable (Figure 1.1). He is famous enough for us to want his signature - or at least buy copies of his plays, tickets to the theatre, to name-check him in 'before-you-die' reading bucket lists - but we also recognise him as a literary torturer who may have ended our love of drama and theatre before it had even begun.

Many books on this subject begin with a chapter about why we should teach Shakespeare. As you will have noticed, so does this one. But while these books are insightful and relevant, many of them start with the basic assumption that you already are convinced of Shakespeare's brilliance. There is a logic to this of course: why would you be holding such a book if it were otherwise? If you are someone with a background in the theatre, or have a passion for literature or performance art, then it is easy to imagine your answer as a resounding cry of "Verily! Bring forth the Bard!" If, on the other hand, your abiding memories of studying, performing or watching Shakespeare's plays are ones of confusion, boredom or embarrassment, then it would be quite understandable if you need more convincing. While we are not shy to share our love of Shakespeare's work, as we will do throughout this book, we are cautiously aware that other people's relationship with Shakespeare could politely be called 'complex'.

So, in this book, we won't presume you are a prior convert, and we make no apologies for this. Yes, you may have come to the idea of teaching Shakespeare willingly, but equally you may be taking the long way around. Either way, we intend to begin by outlining some of the reasons of why teaching Shakespeare is worth it.

The 'problem' with the classics

Shakespeare: classic. Those two words, seemingly inseparable, explain both the appeal and the 'problem' with reading, performing and teaching Shakespeare. Since the 19th century, Shakespeare's status has been elevated from that of famous playwright - a status achieved

DOI: 10.4324/9781003023944-3

Figure 1.1 A portrait of William Shakespeare by Martin Droeshout (1623) used on the cover of the first printed collection of his plays, the *First Folio*.

in his day – to the pinnacle of British (or rather, English) literary achievement. He is a genius, the view goes, with a legacy to be admired by all, a bust on the professor's desk. It is the same thinking that has continued to make Shakespeare a staple of school and university curricula both in Britain and around the world. It is the same thinking that saw English Victorian colonialist adventurers such as Henry Morton Stanley and John Hanning Speke travel across the African interior with a copy of Shakespeare's complete works tucked into their saddle bags. Like the wizard Prospero in *The Tempest* trying to educate and civilise the island native Caliban, Shakespeare represented the lamp of civilisation, of beauty carried into the darkness (Wilson-Lee, 2016).

It is this civilising, or culturing, appeal that makes Shakespeare and other 'classic' texts attractive to educational reformers. Indeed, over the last ten years, reforms of primary education in England have witnessed a renewed determination that children study 'quality' texts with a specific focus on appreciating Britain's "rich and varied literary heritage" (DfE, 2013, p. 13). This has meant a return to classrooms for Shakespeare alongside others in this category: *Little Women*, *The Secret Garden*, *Black Beauty*, *Beowulf* and others. This goes hand in hand with Ofsted's revised *School Inspection Handbook*, which controversially prioritises 'cultural capital' (Ofsted, 2019, p. 43), a move designed to expose disadvantaged children to cultural knowledge deemed important. It is a move its critics have dismissed as an attempt to embed an elitist interpretation of what quality in culture looks like, alienating the very groups it is intended to help (Mansell, 2019).

While good teachers have always sought to offer children quality literature, the mood of this reform is part of a larger shift to promote British culture and intellectual achievement. Since 2014, schools in England are required to promote what the UK government Department for Education calls "fundamental British values" (DfE, 2013), intended to tighten up the standards on spiritual, moral, social and cultural development of pupils to embed a sense of national identity in order to ward off Islamic extremism. In this context, Shakespeare is appealing to schools as it can satisfy both the need for 'quality' and 'Britishness'. Yet, this misappropriation of British cultural symbols to stand for harder to define values is not always a comfortable fit (Hunter-Henin and Vincent, 2018). We are not in any way suggesting that Shakespeare's legacy as an English writer should not inspire pride in children, but simply to recognise the way Shakespeare is used, often inappropriately, as a powerful brand used to stand for and promote a vague sense of an 'authentic' British identity (this is just as popular outside the UK where Shakespeare remains a mark of sophistication, high education and ambition, especially in former British territories).

The inconvenient truth is that Shakespeare wrote not for posterity, but for ordinary people; not for longevity, but in order to put food on the table and make his living. Although the elite of Elizabethan and Jacobean London certainly enjoyed his plays and patronised his theatre company, Shakespeare's plays were mass popular entertainment enjoyed by people of all classes. Yet, in the 21st century, the imperative to teach Shakespeare still too often comes from this place of aspiration. The plays of Mr William Shakespeare are accepted as a byword for 'quality', like a literary gold standard – which they are, but as we will explore in this book, perhaps not for the reasons some might imagine.

While we wholeheartedly celebrate children reading a range of interesting and rich texts both for pleasure and learning, aspiration is the wrong reason to study Shakespeare. Separating out literature into 'classics' and 'fripperies', dividing the canonical texts from the comics, the 'must-reads' and 'never-agains' is at cross-purposes with what it means to be a reader. Readers, especially young ones, are poorly served by learning to see literature as a hierarchy with comic books at the bottom and the pantheon of classics at the top. Instead, we feel passionately that literature should be presented to children as something to be enjoyed, to be actively engaged with, and a route to further curiosities. And that, perhaps surprisingly, is how we see Shakespeare fitting in best of all.

Why study Shakespeare?

As we will explore throughout this book, it is not the man, the myth, the legend – the *Shakespeare* – that matters. As we know from personal experience, when unquestioning deference is the starting point, studying Shakespeare can be a confusing, complicated and bewildering task. We have worked hard to avoid this, to blow the proverbial cobwebs off the Shakespeare statue in order to make it a living, breathing experience for children.

The lineage of stories

Although Shakespeare was writing 400 years ago, it is wrong to think of his writing marooned in the past. Instead, we should think of him as part of the evolving lineage of stories – a literary bloodline that continues to the present. This is important because it also reveals how Shakespeare himself wrote. Many of his plays borrowed heavily from existing stories; some were simply updated versions. *Macbeth* was drawn from Raphael Holinshed's 1587 page-turner *Chronicles of England, Scotland and Ireland; Romeo and Juliet* was lifted from Arthur Brooke's 1562 poem *The Tragicall Historye of Romeus and Juliet*, itself a translation of an earlier work. But the borrowing didn't stop when Shakespeare died: the DNA of many of his stories has found its way into modern films, books and television programmes. *The Lion King*, for example, is a reworking of *Hamlet*; its sequel *The Lion King II: Simba's Pride* leans heavily on *Romeo and Juliet*. There are references to Shakespeare in *SpongeBob Square Pants, The Simpsons* and *Toy Story 3*. Even sci-fi blockbuster *Star Wars* with its secret twins (*Twelfth Night*), informative ghosts (*Hamlet*), fallen tyrants (*Julius Caesar, Macbeth*) and hidden lovers (*Romeo and Juliet*) owes a debt to Shakespeare's works.

While Shakespeare was not shy to plunder works by other authors for good material, his versions are somewhat definitive: nobody is talking about Matteo Bandello's original tragic poem of *Romeus and Juliet*. His gift with language, the iconic set-pieces, the archetypal characters: Shakespeare's plays are rollicking entertainment. Even contemporaries such as Christopher Marlowe or Benjamin Jonson who were prolific and highly respected have not managed to maintain widespread popular appeal. Learning about Shakespeare and his plays is to begin to see how the lineage of stories connects past and present.

Lessons on the human experience

Perhaps what sets Shakespeare apart is how his plays touch on themes so universal that they transcend age, class, time and geography. As we discuss in Chapter 2, he has something to say about our relationships, our feelings, our worries that can still touch us in the 21st century. Michael Rosen recalls a young child once saying they liked how Shakespeare "gets to the big stuff, really quickly" (BBC Teach, 2021). The 'big stuff' is death, life, war, rivalry, love and all the rest. As this child understood, Shakespeare shows us that the people of the past laughed, worried, argued and cried about the same things that we do.

As they read Shakespeare, children will meet characters who love and lie, act nobly and cheat, argue and establish firm friendships; many of these characters they will recognise from other stories and, for better or worse, from their own lives. It helps us understand a little better the experience of being a human. As journalist Yuan Yang neatly puts it, "[i]n many classrooms around the world, it is Shakespeare who breaks the bad news" about human failings (Yang, 2018). Perhaps Shakespeare gets his edge by forcing us to be active, to ask questions about why people behave the way they do and, in doing so, how they can tell us something rather interesting about ourselves and what it means to be a person in this world (Smith, 2020).

Playfulness with language

While much is made of Shakespeare's contribution to the English language in the form of new words coined or quotable lines penned (as discussed in Chapter 2), Shakespeare's joyful playfulness with language is what marks him as a great writer. He is a role model for all children who love the sound and feel of words. His writing sings with slang words, unusual expressions, regional phrases and colourful insults that children love to throw at each other:

Lead apes in hell thou fusty, fly-bitten clack-dish! Patterns and rhymes and word play – all features of Shakespeare's writing – share characteristics with poetry, rap music, playground chants, puns and jokes and are the foundations of getting children excited about language (CLPE, 2019). Even those turns of phrase we use every day – 'wouldn't budge an inch', 'dull as ditch-water', 'my own flesh and blood' – all owe their existence to Shakespeare.

Developing rich and varied vocabulary is a core aim of the Programme of Study for English in the National Curriculum (2013), and Shakespeare offers children a wide range of new and interesting words to play with. Celebrating this love of language can only support a child's interest in reading. After all, reading for pleasure doesn't start with sitting down with a book: it starts with a love of words.

Shakespeare's imprint

As well as speaking *about* our lives, Shakespeare speaks *in* our lives, often without us realising. Such is the ubiquity of Shakespearean references in our cultural space that not being able to pick up on these means to miss out on subtle messaging. "[The United States of America] seemed to bestride the world like a colossus," says the political journalist quoting a line from *Julius Caesar* (Garton Ash, 2020); as does the sports writer who suggests "Et tu, Brute?" as an appropriate question for an Italian football manager facing the sack from his chairman (BBC Sport, 2004); political unrest is described as a "Shakespearean tragedy" (Bader, 2019). His characters are so iconic they have become cultural touchstones for people or characters we love, fear and loathe, and understanding these subtle references can add extra layers of enjoyment and understanding. When you catch the references to forbidden lovers in, for example, Philip Pullman's *His Dark Materials* books, we might be reminded of Romeo and Juliet, and already we know it won't end happily ever after for Lyra and Will.

Although we do not advocate for teaching Shakespeare out of cultural aspiration, such is the extent to which Shakespeare is imprinted on our cultural life that a reader can easily miss these subtle nods or winks without familiarity to Shakespeare's characters and motifs. As will be discussed in Chapter 2, our approach is firmly guided by a need to make Shakespeare relevant to all children's lived experiences, and by advocating for a child-led approach, we recognise that learner and teacher alike have something to bring to a discussion of Shakespeare's plays.

And yet . . .

We are, however, in no doubt that teaching Shakespeare as part of primary literacy is a challenge. Archaic language, complicated themes and grisly plots may seem to present too great and too mature a challenge for the primary years. Others may find the idea of children studying *Macbeth* an example of education being out of step with children's interests, how they learn and interact with each other. In an age where the richness and variety of children's literature is staggering, shouldn't more contemporary and representative authors such as Neil Gaiman, Jasbinder Bilan or Shaun Tan be promoted instead? These are questions we have given serious thought to both in our teaching of Shakespeare and in the writing of this book. But while the technical challenges are real, none are insurmountable. Such is the ubiquity of Shakespeare in the world that knowing him and his works can only contribute to children's wider cultural appreciation.

Teaching Shakespeare through, across and beyond the curriculum

To teach Shakespeare is to teach knowledge. The sheer range of sophisticated knowledge seemingly at his fingertips – warfare, politics, medicine, ancient history, folklore, geography, religious practices and the rest of it – is a monumental achievement. It has given currency to a fringe belief that Shakespeare was in fact *several* geniuses. It is a conspiracy theory that has very little evidence going for it, beyond the snobbish disbelief that a young, relatively uneducated playwright could have produced such heavyweight pieces of literature. It does, however, draw attention to his versatility of plot, setting and theme, which presents teachers of all experiences with a range of jumping-off points to explore other areas of the curriculum alongside language and literature.

Through the curriculum

For most teachers, a study of Shakespeare will find a natural fit in teaching through the core curriculum for English. We deal with this in detail in Chapter 3 (reading, drama and writing). In Appendix 1, we have detailed how each play meets the literacy objectives of the English National Curriculum (2013) for each year group.

It is enough to say here that teaching Shakespeare brings together the threads of the English programme of study in ways other texts might not. In reading, children are challenged with decoding a range of familiar and unfamiliar words, as well as sharpening their skills of critical, collaborative reading comprehension as children make meaning from his imagery and themes, as well as understanding characters and their actions. His plays are rich with unusual and interesting vocabulary.

This goes hand in hand with children's development in oracy: speaking, listening, debating and drama build children's confidence and competence in conventions of performance. Adopting and sustaining roles and understanding the artistic practices of drama – key aims of the curriculum – are essential parts of bringing Shakespeare to life.

Just as Shakespeare was inspired by stories to feed his work as an author, so too can this inspire children in responding to his plays through writing. As we explore in Chapter 3 and throughout Part 2 of this book, his plays are ideal starting points for composing across genres and forms, for a range of purposes and audiences, enhanced by the use of film and interactive platforms for digital storytelling.

Across the curriculum

For teachers planning a wider unit of work based on Shakespeare, his plays can sit comfortably at the heart of a cross-curricular topic. Reading and understanding a play like *The Tempest* will draw on skills and knowledge from across the curriculum – music, dance, artistic skills, English language and geography – and apply them to building understanding of the events on Prospero and Caliban's island. By exploring the rich contexts of each play, the children will be in a far more informed position to understand why these plays were written and how the plots and characters can be understood. Studying the history of the Roman Empire and Republic, for example, gives context to *Julius Caesar*, giving children a better idea of why Julius Caesar is the villain of the piece, not just the victim.

Throughout the chapters in Part 2, we have tried to offer meaningful opportunities to link Shakespeare to the wider work across the English National Curriculum. We have purposefully been selective as the most effective cross-curricular work rests on meaningful rather than tangential links between subjects. Meeting objectives for art, design and technology, music and dance are most obvious in the context of putting on a performance, but RE, history, PSHE and even science can be explored through studying Shakespeare's plays.

Beyond the curriculum

Our approach to teaching Shakespeare, however, aims to take children beyond the limitations of the National Curriculum. Core areas that we feel are essential elements of a 21st-century education – aesthetics, creativity, active learning and digital storytelling – are either absent or receive scant mention in the National Curriculum: a jarring and curious omission for a document that aims to prepare children to live and work in a rapidly changing society. We discuss digital storytelling in Chapter 2, but here we would like to briefly explore the other three areas we feel are essential to working with Shakespeare and in understanding the visual arts in the 21st century.

Aesthetics

The word 'aesthetics' comes from the Greek *αἰσθητικός*, meaning 'beauty', and an aesthetic experience is one where the senses are stimulated with music, speech, light and movement. The feeling that you are there, experiencing it live, is a powerful one. If you've ever been to a raucous pantomime, attended a spectacular live concert or been a part of the crowd as the winning goal in a football match is smashed into the net, then you will know what aesthetics are all about. Yet aesthetic appreciation, so central to how we experience art and culture, is absent from the English National Curriculum.

Bringing different art forms together, rather than placing them in silos, can show children how the arts can be combined to create a visual, aesthetic spectacle. The use of musical instruments and sound effects, as Shakespeare's audiences would have experienced, can add mood and atmosphere to a scene of drama. Experimenting with performing in light and dark, performing outside or on a stage, using simple props and costumes: these are all ways of heightening the sensory experience of storytelling. As the plays are driven almost completely by dialogue with very few stage directions or acting prompts, children are invited to make decisions about the aesthetics of a scene when it is performed (e.g. how lines are delivered, what kind of music will accompany the performance, the seating of the audience). This might seem like a small thing, but it can be a powerful and new experience for many children. After the banging of a big stick on the floor to signal the start of a performance, we have seen classes of tough Year 6 children stunned to silence by the improvised exchanges of the heated, fatal confrontation of Tybalt and Romeo.

Creativity

Shakespeare is perfect for allowing creativity to grow and flourish in your classroom. It presents opportunities for *teaching creatively*: introducing the stories to make a memorable experience or breaking down the themes of complex plays with young children requires all of a teacher's artistry. But crucially, it also allows you to *teach for creativity*: presenting children with challenges and opportunities to ask 'what if?' and explore possibilities, and recognising their agency to make meaningful decisions about how they tell stories (Craft, 2010). As we talk about in Chapter 2, it is the ambiguous, 'gappy' quality of Shakespeare's writing that invites children to begin thinking and working creatively.

Interpreting scenes such as the moments of confrontation in *Romeo and Juliet*, or deciding how flawed characters such as King Leontes from *The Winter's Tale* should be portrayed through drama, requires children to actively negotiate and collaborate with one another to bring the characters to life. This collaborative approach mirrors the same practices used by Shakespeare and his fellow actors as they rehearsed at the Globe Theatre four centuries ago.

When Shakespeare borrowed his storylines from previous works, he wasn't afraid to take liberties with the plots. He changed endings for characters and rewrote villains into heroes. Banquo, for example, was originally an accomplice of Macbeth in the murder of King Duncan, but as King James I was a distant relation, the character was given a more noble role. Challenging the children to write an alternative ending to a play – to walk off the edge of the page – is an opportunity for creative writing. Reimagining a play where (spoiler alert) the lovers don't die, the action is transposed from ancient Rome to a school in present-day Bolton, reversing gender roles so that Juliet ditches Romeo and Tybalt to sort these matters out for herself: these are golden opportunities for teachers and learners alike to explore the writer's craft, admire the effect it has on an audience and then ask the most important question of all: where shall we take this next?

Active learning

Getting children moving, mixing and making with each other in a safe environment makes learning Shakespeare an active, social activity. As we recalled in our experiences of Shakespeare in the introduction to this book, it cannot all be done sitting at a desk. We don't want children to simply 'admire' works of literature: we want children to pick them up and shake them hard.

Performing Shakespeare not only encourages participation, but actively demands it. Children can be active in bringing their experiences and imaginations to bear on how the character will speak, move and look. Behind the stage, children can play the part of directors or manage sound effects – literally taking control of aesthetics of a performance in ways they may have found difficult with other literacy projects.

Inviting children to step forward and take ownership over the learning doesn't mean letting them do whatever they like or leaving lessons unstructured. Shakespeare can be made relevant to younger readers only by letting them infuse it with their own cultural references (and yes, their own cultural capital), in-jokes and, of course, personal insights to modern (adult) life that are usually out of reach of a teacher over the age of 25. This does, however, require the teacher to be willing to take a step back – something that isn't always easy, especially when time is tight and progress is expected. Encouraging active learning not only secures the children's involvement: it also gives a more authentic experience of what it means to put on a performance.

Case study: making the film *Julia Caesar* (2017)

Stefan made the film *Julia Caesar* with a group of Year 4 children as the culmination of a six-part creative writing workshop at a primary school in northern England. He had intended to make a film with the children, but unlike in previous workshops, he made a conscious decision not to decide on the plot for this film in advance but instead to work on the children's responses and draw the ideas from them.

After reading the script for the scene where Caesar is stabbed by the senators, one of the children made the connection that he had been betrayed by some of his friends, notably Brutus. Working on this idea, Stefan asked the children if they had ever felt a similar sense of a friend letting them down, albeit in a less bloodthirsty way! The conversation about what it was like to fall out with friends led Stefan to ask the children if they could think of how this scene might look if it was set in their school and if all the characters were children. Together, they wrote out some of the key features of *Julius Caesar* and tried to find parallels in their school life: Caesar was a bit of a show-off, Brutus his best mate who he hangs around with at playtime, the Forum – an ancient meeting place – became the dining room, the prophecy about the Ides of March might come by text message. One boy suggested that the Roman Senate was a bit like their school council where the pupils make decisions about their school.

And that was the lightbulb moment for the group, and we had a loose, parallel plot to work from: Julia Caesar was on the school council with Brutus, Mark Antony and the others. After trying to take over the council, she was finally put in her place by her 'friends' who threw food on her in the dinner hall. But rather than leave Caesar dead, Stefan asked the children to think about how the conflict might be resolved peacefully and restore the friendship, which helped us write the final scene together where Caesar and his friends are reconciled with the help of a teacher (and they are all in trouble for throwing the food around).

This project was interesting for several reasons, the first being that the children bought into the idea that they had authorial power to play with the storyline, and it gave Stefan pause for thought about to what extent he should pre-determine the direction of his writing workshops. This is the essence of nurturing children's creativity. The second was that the appearance of the video camera added purpose to the children's rehearsals. This was no longer a literacy lesson; this was a film set, and with their classmates set to watch the film when it was ready, the children actively took on roles as actors, directors and producers with as much seriousness as the role of their character. Finally, it showed that a 400-year-old play detailing a 2000-year-old political drama still had something to say to children in the 21st century. Like many of Shakespeare's plays, the plots and characters are still around us. With a small mental leap, we can find plenty of points where Shakespeare's world intersects with our own.

Watch *The Rise and Fall of Julia Caesar* at www.articulateeducation.co.uk/p/gallery.html

Chapter 1: final thoughts

We started this chapter with a question: why study Shakespeare in primary school? True, it is a well-worn question, but it still is worth asking, especially if you are unsure that it is something worth doing. Before we go further, we hope we have convinced you that it is. By setting aside the idea that we should teach Shakespeare in schools either out of habit, aspiration, or out of deference to an author we have *heard* we should respect as serious teachers and readers, we hope to present a way of teaching Shakespeare differently.

Teaching Shakespeare's plays to your children offers a chance for them to be active and creative, and to experience the powerful aesthetics of preparing, watching and performing live storytelling. As they do so, they will meet characters, dilemmas and scenarios that resonate with their own lives, perhaps in surprising ways. If nothing else, we can almost guarantee classrooms filled with laughter and enjoyment. And for the teacher, we have shown that studying Shakespeare is a full educational workout which helps meet core objectives for the English National Curriculum but also moves beyond it. In the next chapter, we will take some of these ideas further to consider how teachers can make Shakespeare relevant to 21st-century learners.

Reading

Further reading

Taylor, G., Jowett, J., Bourus, T. and Egan, G. (Eds.) (2016) *New Oxford Shakespeare: The Complete Works*, Oxford: Oxford University Press.
Wilson-Lee, E. (2016) *Shakespeare in Swahililand: Adventures with the Ever-Living Poet*, London: William Collins.

Online resources

www.bl.uk/shakespeare   The **British Library** offers an excellent variety of resources about Shakespeare's characters, themes and plots. Readers can also take a virtual look at the *First Folio* of Shakespeare's plays.
www.shakespeareweek.org.uk/resources/   **Shakespeare Week** is an annual celebration of Shakespeare's life and works, usually held in March. Their website offers a range of cross-curricular teaching resources.

References

Bader, J. A. (2019) 'The Story of Hong Kong Is a Shakespearean Tragedy' [ONLINE] Available at: www.brookings.edu/blog/order-from-chaos/2019/09/16/the-story-of-hong-kong-is-a-shakespearean-tragedy/ [Accessed 1 December 2020].
BBC Sport (2004) '"Dead Man" Ranieri Walks Tall' [ONLINE] Available at: http://news.bbc.co.uk/sport2/hi/football/teams/c/chelsea/3757825.stm [Accessed 1 December 2020].
BBC Teach (2021) 'Michael Rosen: Why Was Shakespeare So Special?' [ONLINE] Available at: www.bbc.co.uk/teach/why-was-shakespeare-so-special/zf6fmfr [Accessed 1 January 2021].
Blackadder: Back & Forth (1999) BBC One, 6 December.
Centre for Literacy in Primary Education (CLPE) (2019) 'Reading for Pleasure: What We Know Works' [ONLINE] Available at: https://clpe.org.uk/sites/default/files/Reading%20for%20Pleasure_0.pdf [Accessed 1 January 2021].
Craft, A. (2010) 'Teaching for Possibility Thinking: What Is It and How Do We Do It?,' *In Learning Matters*, Volume 15, Issue 1, pp. 19-23.

Department for Education [DfE] (2013) 'Promoting Fundamental British Values as Part of SMSC in Schools' [ONLINE] Available at: www.gov.uk/government/news/guidance-on-promoting-british-values-in-schools-published [Accessed 1 December 2020].

Garton Ash, T. (2020) 'What Will President Biden's United States Look Like to the Rest of the World?,' *The Guardian*, 7 November [ONLINE] Available at: www.theguardian.com/commentisfree/2020/nov/07/what-will-president-bidens-united-states-look-like-to-the-rest-of-the-world [Accessed 1 January 2021].

Hunter-Henin, M. C. and Vincent, C. (2018) 'The Problem with Teaching "British Values" in School,' *The Conversation*, 6 February [ONLINE] Available at: https://theconversation.com/the-problem-with-teaching-british-values-in-school-83688 [Accessed 1 January 2021].

Mansell, W. (2019) 'Ofsted Plan to Inspect "Cultural Capital" in Schools Attacked as Elitist' [ONLINE] Available at: www.theguardian.com/education/2019/sep/03/ofsted-plan-inspect-cultural-capital-schools-attacked-as-elitist [Accessed 1 December 2020].

Ofsted (2019) 'The School Inspection Handbook' [ONLINE] Available at: https://www.gov.uk/government/publications/school-inspection-handbook-eif [Accessed 1 January 2021].

Smith, E. (2020) *This Is Shakespeare: How to Read the World's Greatest Playwright*, London: Pelican.

Wilson-Lee, E. (2016) *Shakespeare in Swahililand: Adventures With the Ever-Living Poet*, London: William Collins.

Yang, Y. (2018) 'The Bard in Beijing: How Shakespeare Is Subverting China,' *Financial Times*, 5 October [ONLINE] Available at: www.ft.com/content/cd997246-c57b-11e8-bc21-54264d1c4647 [Accessed 1 January 2021].

2 Shakespeare and 21st-century education

As we discussed in Chapter 1, the debates about the place of heritage literature in education is misleadingly divisive; appending the word 'classic' to 'literature' raises complex questions about cultural worth and relevance. This is one of the most powerful arguments *against* teaching Shakespeare: he was a man of his time, writing for audiences of one city, in one country in the late 16th and early 17th century. The children we teach have never known anything but the 21st.

Much has been said and written about 21st-century education, and we should be careful not to misconstrue it as simply futuristic education, where digital technology replaces books. Instead, we should see 21st-century education in terms of rights, voice, representation, agency, empathy and equipping learners with the creative skills and knowledge to live and learn in a fast-changing present and an uncertain future. Of course, this should give educators pause for thought about how we define literacy and how we view the role of literature in enabling this transition (Luna Scott, 2015; Davies, Newton and Newton, 2018; Gill, Kucharczyk and Lenahan, 2021). Using Shakespeare to meet these needs is not without challenges, but, as we will show, it is not without immense reward.

This chapter has three aims:

- To outline approaches for reading meaning into Shakespeare's plays
- To show how 21st-century learners can find meaning in Shakespeare's writing
- To show how teaching Shakespeare in primary literacy is relevant to 21st-century teaching

Was Shakespeare 'of an age' or 'for all time'?

Perhaps more than other forms of art, writing is steeped in the era it was written. Language (syntax, vocabulary, spelling, meaning), content (current affairs, satire, political references) and themes (accepted stereotypes of gender, race and difference in particular) can seem to root a piece of writing in a specific era. In the *First Folio*, the first collected works of Shakespeare printed by his associates in 1623 after his death, Shakespeare's work is described as being 'for all time'. Although Shakespeare was certainly famous and respected in his day, he wrote for his times not with immortality in mind. It is easy to see how an audience at the Globe Theatre might have heard echoes of 1605's foiled Gunpowder Plot while watching *Macbeth*, or understood the negative racial stereotypes present in *Othello* or *The Merchant of*

DOI: 10.4324/9781003023944-4

Venice. In the 21st century, modern social movements such as Black Lives Matter and #MeToo have rightly forced us to reappraise how gender, race and issues of inclusion are presented in education. The Royal Shakespeare Company appears to recognise this too, pledging to extend diversity of gender and race to its productions (Terry, 2017). But Shakespeare's treatment of these themes may give us pause for thought when thinking of how we might communicate this to young children.

If teachers recognise the need for inclusive, representative literature, should they bother with Shakespeare at all? And if they choose to use his plays to interrogate those themes, is Shakespeare up to it? Is he really a 'universal' author, someone whose ideas are timeless and can span generational divide?

In the next part of this chapter, we will explore how we feel Shakespeare's works can be made relevant to young readers and learners.

Exploring the gaps: making Shakespeare relevant

Reverence for classic texts, especially ones written in archaic or ancient languages, can make us feel that in order to understand them, they need to be deciphered rather than read: meaning and hidden wisdom, buried deep within the lines, can be extracted by a worthy reader.

Part of this relates to language. Unlike texts such as *Beowulf* – written in **Old English** and in need of translation for the majority of readers – Shakespeare's plays are written in **early modern English**: similar in both grammar and syntax to English spoken today (Crystal, 2008). We will discuss this further in Chapter 3. Admittedly, that is not the popular perception, and we accept that readers for whom English is an additional language or those with reading impairments might find some of his writing inaccessible. But the idea that Shakespeare's writing is 'out of reach' of most readers reinforces exclusionary myths about classic literature.

A further issue is about our right as readers to challenge and reinterpret classic texts. The National Curriculum for England compounds this idea by expecting pupils to 'appreciate' fiction of our literary heritage – as one might appreciate a priceless Ming vase in a museum case – rather than 'understand' it (DfE, 2013). This implies, wrongly in our view, that reading is a one-way street where only the reader is changed by reading a text. Reading Shakespeare, especially for younger children, should not be about slavishly trying to decipher 'truth' from his words. We feel strongly that these plays should not be read for what Shakespeare said *then*, but for what it says to us *in the here and now*. What Shakespeare says about love in *A Midsummer Night's Dream* is only important if we use it to examine our own lives: how and who we love, the relationships that are important to us.

We offer three interesting approaches on reading Shakespeare and reading in general that we feel should shape every practitioner's approach to teaching Shakespeare.

Gappiness

Shakespeare scholar Emma Smith argues that it is the "gappy quality" that makes Shakespeare's work worth reading and studying (Smith, 2020, p. 2). Ambiguity about characters, plot holes and the lack of stage directions allows readers to actively participate in the reading of a Shakespeare play. It encourages us, Smith suggests, to challenge established ideas about how a character *should be* played, or how lines *ought to be* read.

It is certainly true that Shakespeare's writing is full of loose threads: unseen off-stage events (Lady Macbeth's death), untold backstories (Leontes' relationship with Hermione in *The Winter's Tale*) and general vagueness (why was Prospero *really* exiled in *The Tempest*?). Pulling at these threads allows us as modern readers to yank the wool into a new shape, so to speak. For Smith, "ambiguity is the oxygen" of Shakespeare's plays (2020, p. 3); whether this was accident or design on his part, it should give educators licence (and confidence) to encourage children to be active, enquiring readers: to poke their fingers into the 'gaps' and wiggle them around as their curiosity takes them.

Rorschach Shakespeare

Anne Coldiron has also explored the flexibility in making meaning from reading texts by proposing the concept of 'Rorschach Shakespeare' (Coldiron, 2008). This takes its name from the Rorschach test: a psychological examination where patients discuss the images they see in random ink-blot patterns. As each viewer sees something different in the ink blots, this may reveal something about the viewer. In the context of the plays, Rorschach Shakespeare implies that meaning is made as much by the viewer as it is by the reader. This makes the reading process a much more personal, much more inviting experience. Take Caliban, the island native from *The Tempest*, as an example. Some see Caliban as an exotic monster; some see him as an oppressed aboriginal man mis-used and mis-understood by his masters. He could be either, and neither view is wrong. Getting children to read Shakespeare in this way not only encourages them to take ownership, but also to recognise that our experiences shape how we read things, and each reader will have a different understanding. We encourage teachers to embrace this.

Transactional theory: a two-way street

Louise Rosenblatt's influential work on a 'transactional theory' of reading (Rosenblatt, 1978) encourages us to see reading as a two-way process: a relationship between the text and the reader. As such, a text such as *Romeo and Juliet*, written in the 1590s, is 'reactivated' when we read it in the 2020s injecting it with our values and understandings of the world. Doing so allows us, for example, to ask questions of Juliet's place in society as a young woman: something important to us in the 21st century which would hardly have registered when it was first performed. As part of a 'transaction', both the reader and the text are manipulated by this exchange. And as we retell the story of *The Tempest*, *The Winter's Tale* and *Macbeth* as comic books, computer games and films – as we very much encourage you to do so – these versions too reshape our collective understanding of the original (Jones, 2010; Coles and Bryer, 2018).

As we described in Chapter 1, the problem with reading 'classic' texts is that we feel meaning should be *extracted* rather than *made*, much in the way you might solve a cryptic crossword puzzle or carry out a painful piece of dentistry. But to view heritage literature as something preserved in the past does not help modern readers. The past is not a mosquito preserved in amber to be admired many years later. As with *Jurassic Park*, the moment of value happens when you reawaken the mosquito, allowing the past to become living and breathing in the present (although it is less likely you will be eaten by Shakespeare).

We feel that the three approaches outlined previously should frame how teachers and children engage with Shakespeare in primary English – an idea we explore further in Chapter 3. Seeing Shakespeare as permissively gappy, inviting us to come to our own conclusions about what we see and read, should be liberating. It has certainly helped us. Forget the puffed-up ideas of 'classic' texts. Treating Shakespeare's writing in this way is not sacrilege: it is what it is designed for.

21st-century boy: making Shakespeare relevant

Educator Rex Gibson argues that it is the emotional, social and personal aspects of Shakespeare's writing that gives it continued relevance in the present day. It is where he finds his immortality. He speaks to us still, Gibson suggests, because Shakespeare was attuned to the things that have always made us human: what he calls "abiding and familiar concerns" (Gibson, 1998). He touches on the big themes that affect our lives: growing up, ambition, love and growing old (Bate, 2016). It is the same reason that theatre and film directors such as Erica Whyman, Nicholas Hynter and Baz Luhrman have all chosen to reposition Shakespeare's stories in the present day. Shakespeare's work is used to shine a light upon themes and issues that still shape modern society.

We would like to draw attention to three key issues that we feel are powerfully relevant to 21st-century learning and how they can be explored by reading Shakespeare. These are **empathy**, **gender** and **race**.

Empathy

"How beauteous mankind is! O brave new world, That has such people in it!" declares Miranda in *The Tempest*. Miranda, daughter of Prospero, is part virginal symbol of purity and a better future to come, part pedigree housecat. She's complex like many of Shakespeare's characters. They are *such people*. One of the greatest rewards of studying literature with children is discussing how they can empathise with the characters they meet and using it as a platform to develop social and emotional intelligence (Kucharczyk and Hanna, 2020). Shakespeare's characters demand our empathy. Although some of their actions and motivations are better understood by adults, that his characters represent the very best, and the very worst of human behaviour, there is plenty here for the children to identify with. Yes, we have heroes and legends (Antony and Cleopatra), great leaders (Caesar) and forces of nature (Emelia in *Othello*). Yet Shakespeare also shows us that people can be weak (Hamlet), treacherous (Macbeth), manipulative (Lady Macbeth), cruel (King Leontes), argumentative (Oberon and Titania), tragic (Romeo and/or Juliet) and just plain idiotic (Trinculo). They pursue and reject, love and murder, honour and cheat one another.

Relationships, for example, are one aspect that children will be certain to identify with. Consider the scene where Mercutio rushes in to save Romeo from Tybalt's blade in *Romeo and Juliet*. Who hasn't tried to stand up for someone they love? Who hasn't waded into an argument with best intentions, only to end up suffering the most (although hopefully not as fatally as Mercutio)? In other stories, we have Prospero as an over-bearing parent to Miranda in *The Tempest* and the betrayal of friendship in *Macbeth* and *Julius Caesar*. These are timeless ideas that will deepen with age and experience, which is one reason why we encourage young children to read Shakespeare. This is the transactional approach to reading at work. How we read the play gives the play meaning. In the process of being active, creative and collaborative, this may even help build closer, more trusting bonds between learners and adults.

Gender

Although it is commonly believed that women were forbidden from performing on stage in Elizabethan and Jacobean England, no specific law prohibiting this has ever been identified (Schiermeister, 2005). Female actors did in fact take to the stage in England, even performing for Elizabeth I at her palace (Brown, 2017). We must assume, then, that Shakespeare deliberately excluded women from the stage, instead choosing to cast men and boys in female roles.

In his plays, as in his society, women were defined by their relationships to men: queens to kings, wives to husbands, mothers to sons, and sisters to brothers. His female characters generally play secondary roles to the men: Cleopatra to Antony, Juliet to Romeo, Lady Macbeth to her husband, and so on.

When teaching Shakespeare to children, we would encourage teachers to be flexible when casting children to characters and encourage them to play the *role* rather than the *gender*. It is hard to avoid, however, that female roles are rather limited: their lives are often unsatisfied, their destinies out of their hands or, often, quite bloody. In *Macbeth*, Lady Macbeth is instrumental in her husband's downfall but disappears mid-play and dies off stage while the spotlight focuses on her husband. Younger children might notice that it is boys who usually take the interesting lead roles (wizard, king, soldier, rescuer) while the girls play supporting roles (daughter, wife, girlfriend). They relish turning this on its head. With older primary children, you can take the conversation further. Does it make a difference that the female roles were written for men to play? Should we blame the female characters for being weak or silent, or the male writer who created them? Do Shakespeare's female characters behave in a believable way? Or are they, as Heather Froehlich has shown, largely there to give the men something to talk about (Froehlich, 2015)?

We hope that these ideas might seem obvious to an adult reader, but this is a conversation that children may never have had before. Doing so touches on an important social issue and reveals more about the intentions of an author.

Activities for discussing Shakespeare and gender with your class

Here are some ideas for how you might begin to challenge and subvert the gender roles within the story.

Gender swap

Experiment in performing key scenes with girls playing the 'boys' parts and vice versa. Focus on how the gender of characters might influence or determine the choices they make. For example, in *Romeo and Juliet*, would Tybalt, Mercutio and Romeo have come to fatal blows if the characters were female? Would Julia Caesar have sought ultimate power or have been more willing to cooperate? Or, would the characters have behaved in exactly the same way? This is a simple idea but a powerful one for exploring gendered behaviour in literature.

The Bechdel Test

Named after American cartoonist Alison Bechdel, the Bechdel Test is a measure of how active and present female characters are in literature and film. To pass the test, a work must feature two named women who have a conversation about anything other than a man or boy (and in other variations, about romance or babies). Discuss this with the children, asking them why they think it is important and what it might say about the things they read and watch. As they read, decide if the play passes the Bechdel Test or not (spoiler: don't get your hopes up!). You might challenge the children to rewrite scenes that do.

Stereotypes

Show the children a list of adjectives describing different character traits: aggressive, loving, funny, brave, beautiful. Ask the children if these words best describe a boy or a girl – no sitting on the fence! In our experience, many (but not all) children can be quick to classify boys as mischievous, aggressive and brave, and girls as loving, caring and friendly. It is good to challenge this, especially when asking children to empathise with certain characters in drama and writing. Ask the children if all the boys (and men) they know fit that description. Do they know girls/women who are aggressive or brave? Do they know men who are loving and good at listening? Doing this can help draw a distinction between expectations of gender and the realities. The same test can be applied to characters the children meet in Shakespeare's stories. For example, are all the men in *Julius Caesar* aggressive hotheads? Cassius is for sure, but Brutus, Mark Antony and even Caesar himself all show more nuanced personal traits.

Race

How race and racial identity are represented in children's literature is a live social issue thanks to Black Lives Matter and other social movements. Children from all backgrounds, but especially those who identify as BAME, are very likely to be aware of these debates but perhaps less certain about how they apply to them, especially about what they read and watch.

Shakespeare's treatment of racial 'others' – namely Othello, who is a black north African in a European royal court, and Caliban from *The Tempest*, who is a native inhabitant of the island – play upon racial stereotypes that were accepted in his time but present challenges for practitioners bringing Shakespeare into multi-racial, multi-ethnic classrooms.

Teachers will have to decide how much they wish to draw attention to race or the lack of racial diversity in his plays (especially the ones chosen in this book) just as black actors wrestle with how much to focus on the race of a character as part of their identity. Perhaps a lack of racial diversity is understandable in *Macbeth* (set in 14th-century Scotland), perhaps less so for *A Midsummer Night's Dream* (set in a magical forest where, as donkey-heads attest, anything and anyone is possible). To consider the role of otherness, in Chapter 4 we have directed teachers towards the role of Caliban in *The Tempest*. Here the island native is presented as a monster, his name a riff on 'cannibal'. Yet Caliban's status can help inform us about the legacy of colonialism and slavery as well as how non-white characters in stories often are presented as exotics or oddities (Ramdarshan Bold, 2019).

It is important, however, for teachers to realise that it is not enough for their classroom to be 'colour-blind'. For some children, even very young ones, racial identity is an integral part of who they feel they are. Validating this by discussing race and literature is important (Gaine, 2005). For literature to be transformative, we encourage teachers to help children transpose the action of Shakespeare's plays to settings and contexts more meaningful to them. If they choose to inject their cultural or ethnic identity into the characters they meet, they are free to do so; if they choose to ignore it, then that is their right.

When we taught *Romeo and Juliet* to a racially diverse class, thinking about what is used to divide people (including race, culture and religion) helped the children understand why the families might want to keep the lovers apart. But equally, when teaching *Julius Caesar* to a different group of children, a powerful discussion about motivation and revenge transcended race and did not impede British, Ethiopian and Libyan conspirators assailing a female, British-Pakistani Caesar. Letting children make decisions about how they learn these stories and not being afraid to encourage them to explore these important issues will reap rewards.

Trading places: Shakespeare reimagined

Watching Shakespeare set in a different cultural context (even in a different language) can show to children how directors and actors interpret Shakespeare's most famous stories.

Josh (Dir. Mansoor Khan, India, 2000)

For *Romeo and Juliet*, watch a clip of *Josh* (India, 2000), a Hindi-language film that swaps the streets of Verona for modern Goa. Chandrachur Singh plays Rahul (Romeo), a Hindu and a member of the Bichoo gang who falls in love with Shirley Dias (Juliet), a member of a rival Christian gang, the Eagles, and played by Aishwarya Rai. Despite Rahul's best efforts to woo Shirley with a box of pastries, Shirley's brother Max (Tybalt), played by heartthrob Shahrukh Khan, stands in their way. The scene where Rahul enters the Eagles' territory is superbly tense.

Watch a clip at: https://youtu.be/kqeSqGdvLno

uMabatha/Zulu Macbeth (Dir. Welcome Msomi, South Africa, 1970)

This story reimagines *Macbeth* as the story of famed Zulu warrior chief Shaka Zulu. Director and writer Welcome Msomi draws on the themes of intrigue, ambition and revenge both to celebrate Shaka and his place in Zulu (and South African) history, but also to demonstrate the play's universal appeal.

Watch a clip at: https://youtu.be/OpECqlUykog

All the world's a stage: making Shakespeare relevant to teaching in the 21st century

As we explained in Chapter 1, we feel that good practice in teaching Shakespeare enables creativity and active learning. By embracing a gappy, Rorschach-shifting, *living* Shakespeare, we encourage teachers to allow children to be active participants in what and how they learn. This means getting up, making decisions, making mistakes and co-constructing understanding of the plays together and hand in hand with the adults they work with. This may seem daunting, especially for newly qualified teachers unsure about where to start, but we feel that creativity, child-centred learning with an emphasis on emotional literacy, child-initiated learning and co-constructed knowledge through collaboration are vital components of a literacy education in the 21st century.

Developments in technology influence how we tell stories. Just as it did for William Shakespeare, technology is changing what it means to be literate (Gill, Kucharczyk and Lenahan, 2021). Whereas we have social media and digital technology, innovators in early modern England had the printing press and the compass. Although the ability to print a book might seem like ancient technology, these inventions expanded boundaries, allowing people to communicate in different ways. Just as virtual reality, multimodal stories, film and immersive computer gaming enhance how we enjoy stories today, playwrights in Shakespeare's era were experimenting with movable stages and even live cannon fire to enhance the visual spectacle (according to one eyewitness, this set-piece certainly achieved its aim as the cannonball set fire to the theatre and it burned to the ground). So, making use of technology to support how children understand, perform and respond to his plays is not just about making it relevant: it is authentically Shakespearean.

We deal with reading, drama and creative writing in Chapter 3. In this section, we outline suggestions for using three technologies to enhance your teaching of Shakespeare: **film**, **digital storytelling** and **digital world building**.

Film: watching and making films about Shakespeare

Shakespeare was in the business of mass popular entertainment. If he were alive today, it wouldn't be a surprise to find him as a writer on *Coronation Street*, on a Hollywood film set directing the award-winning *Romeo and Juliet Trilogy* or experimenting with virtual reality and 3D.

Watching a film adaptation alongside a text can be an effective way of making Shakespeare accessible for children, and in Part 2 we have suggested suitable adaptations to support children's understanding of the plays (see also Box 2.2 in Chapter 2). If time is short, and you choose to focus on one key scene – for example, the assassination of Julius Caesar – then a film adaptation can provide the full story arc and the context for 'the before' and 'the after' of your chosen scene.

But watching film is more than simply a means of engaging the children: showing them how to critically discuss visual and digital media is about equipping them with the skills to be literate in the 21st century (Parry, 2013). Drawing their attention to how characters are arranged on the screen (*mise en scène*), the choice of camera shot and the effect of lighting can tell us a lot about how a director wants us to see a character, a moment of action or a setting. This in turn can add a cinematic quality to children's writing. They can visualise how Macbeth stares fatefully into the distance as Burnham Wood approaches under darkening skies, or how the kindly shepherd goes through agonies about whether or not to pick up Perdita's basket in *The Winter's Tale* because they will have seen it or staged it.

Getting children to *make* their own films puts children in the position to actively reimagine a story for a different media, making creative choices in collaboration with other children. Making a film is not just about the product. The decision making about music and sound, camera angles, an actor's body language and voice, costumes, props and setting all add to the children's understanding of a story. This puts the skills learned in drama to a practical, purposeful use.

It can help children see how a character interacts with the setting which, when they come to write descriptively, allows them to add a cinematic quality to writing. It also attunes children to think about 'composing' a narrative with purpose for a specific audience. While composing for a film might be wordless, of course children will also be writing scripts for characters to read aloud, which adds the additional challenge of telling a story only through character dialogue.

Although teachers may have misgivings about the skills required to support children in filmmaking, it can be achieved with basic equipment most schools in the UK already have access to, such as cameras, tablets and computers. Basic video-editing software such as *Windows Movie Maker* and *iMovies* are all free and usable by primary-aged children.

Resources for watching films (including Shakespeare) and making films with children can be found at: www.thefilmspace.org and www2.bfi.org.uk/education-research

Digital storytelling

Stop-motion is a form of film animation. Although it is a technique as old as cinema itself, it has been popularised in modern culture by filmmaker Nick Park and his *Wallace and Gromit*

movies. Rather than moving footage being captured with a video camera, the illusion of movement is created by photographing and then gradually moving solid objects, such as puppets, poseable action figures or images cut from paper. 'Motion' is then created by showing the series of still photographs in quick succession. The technology required is quite simple (a camera, a stage, some moveable characters, free video-editing software). As a storytelling tool, it is deeply immersive, and as animators, children have complete creative control to make authorial choices that can add to a narrative and be built on in writing lessons.

For more on making stop-motion films, *Stop Motion: Passion, Process and Performance* by Barry Purves (2019) is comprehensive guidance on the art form for adults. *The Lego Animation Book* (Pagano and Pickett, 2016) is ideal for getting younger readers started.

Scratch animation (www.scratch.mit.edu) is a free animation platform that allows users to create games, movies and interactive adventures. Many schools use this platform already to help children understand the basics of coding. This platform offers versatility for storytelling as children can reimagine aspects of Shakespeare's stories as puzzles and interactive games. As well as embedding aspects of the stories, this allows children to concentrate on the aesthetics of their creation: sound, pace and visual effects.

Twine (www.twinery.org) is an online platform for creative branching story narratives suitable for upper KS2. Similar to choose-your-own-adventure books, authors can create short narratives with multiple options at key moments, giving the reader the choice to change the route, and thus the outcome, of the story. This is ideal for exploring character dilemmas (will Brutus change his mind and let Caesar live?) and imagining alternate endings (Juliet wakes up before Romeo kills himself; Perdita is raised by bears rather than a shepherd).

Digital world building

Minecraft

The popular computer game *Minecraft* is a computer-based world-building game where players have the freedom to create a virtual environment from scratch and populate the world with animated characters. This can be played on a screen or using a VR headset. Each world can be built alone or in collaboration with other builders. It is relatively simple and can be used by even very young children with a large degree of independence.

Many have already recognised the educational potential of *Minecraft* as an ideal platform for incubating story ideas in the pre-writing stage (Bindel, n.d.). The children can create characters to enter this world and tell the story as their characters explore it. Using *Minecraft* to recreate Macbeth's castle with the surrounding gloomy heathland helps children to get a sense of tone, mood and atmosphere so vital to understanding the play. This might be true to the original story or might allow them to take the story into more imaginative places.

Chapter 2: final thoughts

Although Shakespeare was writing more than four centuries ago, his plays retain a timeless quality. His complex characters demand our empathy, and their tragic flaws and noble heroics feel immediate and real. But making sense of them requires us to forget a lot of what we think we know about Shakespeare. The plays can only really have meaning – are only 'reactivated' – when read in the present set against the context of our own lives and experiences. The plays can be used as a context to have complex discussions about empathy, gender, race and otherness. This is the best way we have found to help children feel a connection with kings and queens, senators, assassins and wizards.

For teachers, this may in fact present a greater challenge than for the children. But we have found that allowing pupils to be active in interpreting characters' motives and actions allows for deeper understanding. Digital technology, an essential component of 21st-century storytelling, is a vehicle to allow children to play with ideas in virtual spaces as well as on stages, pages and filmsets. Shakespeare is only 'for all time' if we make it so.

Reading

Suggested reading

Gill, A., Kucharczyk, S. and Lenahan, C. (2021) 'Reading and Children's Lives,' in A. Gill, M. Stephenson and D. Waugh (Eds.) *Developing a Love of Reading and Books*, London: Sage.
Smith, E. (2020) *This Is Shakespeare: How to Read the World's Greatest Playwright*, London: Pelican.

Online resources

http://cargocollective.com/chickenshopshakespeare **Chicken Shop Shakespeare** is a Shakespeare project based in northern England that stages scenes from Shakespeare's plays in fried chicken shops around Leeds.
https://core-cms.bfi.org.uk/media/4673/download 'Moving images in the classroom: Teaching basic techniques' is an excellent free publication from the **British Film Institute (BFI)** about how to teach children to 'read' films.
https://tinkerlab.com/easy-stop-motion-animation-kids/ This blogpost from **TinkerLab** outlines a simple approach to starting with stop-motion animation.
https://warwick.ac.uk/fac/arts/english/research/currentprojects/multiculturalshakespeare **The British Black and Asian (BBA) Shakespeare** project based at the University of Warwick aims to map the history of non-white actors' and directors' role in bringing Shakespeare to screen and stage. It offers a range of videos, images and information about actors.

References

Bate, J. (2016) '"The Infirmity of His Age": Shakespeare's 400th Anniversary,' *The Lancet (British Edition)*, Volume 387, Issue 10029, pp. 1715–1716.
Bindel, A. (n.d.) *Building in Minecraft Is a Lot Like . . . Writing?* [ONLINE] Available at: https://tocaboca.com/magazine/minecraft-sandbox-storytelling/ [Accessed 1 October 2020].
Brown, P. A. (2017) 'Why Did the English Stage Take Boys for Actresses?,' *Shakespeare Survey*, Volume 70, pp. 182–187.
Coldiron, A. E. B. (2008) 'Canons and Cultures: Is Shakespeare Universal?,' in Laurie Maguire (Ed.) *How to Do Things with Shakespeare: New Approaches, New Essays*, London: Blackwell.
Coles, J. and Bryer, T. (2018) 'Reading as Enactment: Transforming Beowulf Through Drama, Film and Computer Game,' *English in Education*, Volume 52, Issue 1, pp. 54–66.
Crystal, D. (2008) *Think on My Words: Exploring Shakespeare's Language*, Cambridge: Cambridge University Press.
Davies, L. M., Newton, L. D. and Newton, D. P. (2018) 'Creativity as a Twenty-First-Century Competence: An Exploratory Study of Provision and Reality,' *Education*, Volume 46, Issue 7, pp. 3–13.
Department for Education (2013) *The National Curriculum in England: Key Stages 1 and 2 Framework Document* [ONLINE] Available at: www.gov.uk/government/publications/national-curriculum-in-england-primary-curriculum [Accessed 1 October 2020].

Froehlich, H. (2015) *Does Shakespeare Pass the Bechdel Test?* [ONLINE] Available at: https://hfroehli. ch/2013/04/04/does-shakespeare-pass-the-bechdel-test/ [Accessed 1 October 2020].

Gaine, C. (2005) *We're All White, Thanks: The Persisting Myth about 'White' Schools*, Stoke-on-Trent: Trentham.

Gibson, R. (1998) *Teaching Shakespeare*, Cambridge: Cambridge University Press.

Gill, A., Kucharczyk, S. and Lenahan, C. (2021) 'Reading and Children's Lives,' in A. Gill, M. Stephenson and D. Waugh (Eds.) *Developing a Love of Reading and Books*, London: Sage.

Jones, C. (2010) 'From Heorot to Hollywood: Beowulf in Its Third Millennium,' in N. Perkins and D. Clark (Eds.) *Anglo-Saxon Culture and the Modern Imagination*, 13–30, Cambridge: Boydell & Brewer.

Kucharczyk, S. and Hanna, H. (2020) 'Balancing Teacher Power and Children's Rights: Rethinking the Use of Picturebooks in Multicultural Primary Schools in England,' *Human Rights Education Review*, Volume 3, Issue 1 (June), pp. 49–68.

Luna Scott, C. (2015) 'The Futures of Learning 2: What Kind of Learning for the 21st Century?,' UNESCO Education Research and Foresight, Paris. [ERF Working Papers Series, No. 14].

Pagano, D. and Pickett, D. (2016) *The Lego Animation Book: Make Your Own Lego Movies!*, San Francisco: No Starch Press.

Parry, B. (2013) *Children, Film and Literacy*, Basingstoke: Palgrave Macmillan.

Purves, B. J. (2019) *Stop-Motion Animation: Frame by Frame Film-Making with Puppets and Models* (2nd Edition), London: Bloomsbury.

Ramdarshan Bold, M. (2019) *Representation of People of Colour among Children's Book Authors and Illustrators: Booktrust Represents (April 2019)*, London: Booktrust.

Rosenblatt, L. (1978) *The Reader, the Text, the Poem: The Transactional Theory of the Literary Work*, Carbondale: Southern Illinois University Press.

Schiermeister, J. (2005) 'The False Issue of Female "Illegality" of Female Performance,' *The Shakespeare Standard* [ONLINE] Available at: http://theshakespearestandard.com/false-issue-illegality-female-performance/ [Accessed 1 October 2020].

Terry, M. (2017) 'New Shakespeare's Globe Chief Promises Far More Diverse Casting,' *The Guardian*, 18 August [ONLINE] Available at: www.theguardian.com/stage/2017/aug/18/new-shakespeares-globe-chief-promises-far-more-diverse-casting-michelle-terry [Accessed 1 October 2020].

3 Words and deeds

Exploring Shakespeare's plays through reading, drama and writing

Teaching Shakespeare in primary school should be a fun, active, social and creative experience. Of course there are challenges in doing this for both teachers and learners: *How do you make the language accessible for younger children? Where do you start with a* play? *How do you use drama as an effective tool for exploring these works?* To answer these questions, this chapter has been divided into two parts. As we are talking about Shakespeare, however, it seems more appropriate to call them two 'acts'.

Act I deals with Shakespeare's 'words' and considers how to read Shakespeare's plays with children and implications for teaching key areas of the English National Curriculum: grammar and syntax, new vocabulary, pronunciation and spelling. Act I will also discuss reading *between* the lines in Shakespeare's plays – understanding his use of imagery – and reading *beyond* the lines and making meaning from his plays. We also discuss considerations for choosing texts to use with your class and the use of film.

Act II turns to 'deeds': how a teacher can use drama effectively to make meaning from the people, places and predicaments of Shakespeare's plays. Act II looks at principles of effective drama teaching, presents a drama 'toolbox' with suggestions for staging Shakespeare in the classroom and suggestions for troubleshooting drama lessons. The act closes by exploring how children can respond to Shakespeare through creative writing in print, on the stage and through digital storytelling.

Act I. Words: reading Shakespeare's plays

Shakespeare was a poet and an entertainer. Reading his words detached from the idea of live performance is only half the experience, and probably the lesser half; his words are meant to be read aloud and performed to an audience. For teachers of primary-aged children, this does present challenges, and careful consideration needs to be given to building children's confidence (and your own!) in making accessible the early modern English that the plays are written in as well as navigating the complexity of Shakespeare's ideas. A challenge, yes, but as we discovered, one that is full of possibility and reward even for teachers with no experience of theatre. How teachers get children to interact with Shakespeare's words will determine the impact your teaching of Shakespeare has on the children and their lasting memories of the experience. In this section, therefore, we will explore ways to overcome these perceived obstacles and share our experiences of introducing Shakespeare to young readers.

DOI: 10.4324/9781003023944-5

The 'daring tongue': Shakespeare's language

Shakespeare's language is one of the most cited issues with teaching Shakespeare to children (Bloom, 2016). The early modern English of Shakespeare's time is so different from our own, the argument goes, that children simply won't understand the words, and it will put them off reading Shakespeare for life. This is a view that many have carried into adulthood from their painful memories of reading Shakespeare at school: wading through dense prose, pulling the wings off the butterfly as they try to find out what it all means (Powell, 2014).

Shakespeare's language *is* unusual to our ears, and it is not always easy to tune into without effort. It is of course more than 400 years old, so it shouldn't be much of a surprise that we find some words obscure or challenging. Think of how Shakespeare himself might have coped with 'supercomputer', 'hashtag' or 'carburettor'. Yet so much of it is rich and exciting, quotable and rhythmic. Shakespeare would be at home in an age where powerful political sloganeering ("Brutus is an honourable man!"), rap music ("Shall I compare thee to a summer's day" can be rapped over most hip-hop songs. Try it.) and short, snappy tweets that trip off the tongue ("To be or not to be. Lol. #thatisthequestion") are the order of the day.

It is also worth remembering two things. Firstly, Shakespeare was not a novelist: he was a poet who wrote plays. As such, his writing is packed full of poetic devices such as imagery, word play and rhythm, all of which add to the **aesthetic** quality, while dispensing with some of the realism. And this leads to the second consideration: as poetry, Shakespeare's language is likely to have challenged his audiences as much as it does us. As they wandered out of the premiere of *Julius Caesar*, they too would have puzzled over certain phrases and images in the tavern afterwards. This should give readers today both comfort and encouragement. After all, discussing what it all means is one of the best things to enjoy about literature.

Certainly, teachers of all experiences will need to consider implications for readers with low confidence or for those who are learning English as an additional language. Yet, making ambitious texts accessible to younger readers is the cornerstone of best practice in English teaching. But we would urge teachers to be brave. Presenting Shakespeare as suitable only for native English speakers and high achievers is to miss the point of who Shakespeare was and reinforces myths that his works are for a highly educated elite rather than universal works that are part of world literary heritage.

To teach children to read Shakespeare's words well, we encourage you to think about these three stages of reading development (Guppy and Hughes, 1999): **reading the lines** (what is actually said and by whom), **reading between the lines** (what it might mean) and, finally, **reading beyond the lines** (why the author chose this language). The sections that follow will show you how.

Reading the lines: speaking Shakespeare's words

Linguist David Crystal challenges the idea that Shakespeare's language is too complex for modern readers. He estimates that only between 5 and 10 percent of Shakespeare's words might provide a problem for pronunciation and comprehension (Crystal, 2008).

As such, he suggests, the need to 'translate' or simplify the text in order for it to be understood is wrong. We too agree that to offer children only modern or simplified versions is to lose the richness, the 'unusualness' that makes Shakespeare's writing sing like poetry.

When asking children to read the words of a Shakespeare script for the first time, we would encourage patience. Allow the children to get a feel for saying the words before trying to understand them. This can be done through call and response between teacher and children to build confidence, experimenting with performance voices and adding actions. When children read a passage aloud, allow them to take turns so they can hear others speaking the same words. During these early readings, we would encourage teachers to resist the urge to correct children or to 'translate' every word. Of course, it is important to help children identify new and unknown vocabulary, but reading his words aloud, even just a few lines of dialogue, can stimulate curiosity in children even if the meaning is still obscure. As you read, reassure them that this is a challenge for you too and they will be OK freewheeling for a few moments. Let them play with the words and look for clues before moving on to deciding what Shakespeare means.

Reading a script

It is unlikely that Shakespeare gave each of the actors in his play a complete script. It would have both been too expensive and time consuming to copy out. Instead, actors would have a cue sheet that contained their lines and, importantly, the last few words of the previous speaker's lines to act as a prompt (Maguire, 2008). Actors like Richard Burbage probably rehearsed alone, and it is testament to the skills of the performers of the day that the plays did not go catastrophically wrong when they were first launched (teachers: for context, try to imagine doing the end-of-year play in this way). Teachers may consider taking lessons from this. Having just a few lines on a piece of paper is far less threatening than having the full script. Relying on the cue lines to know when to step in will help keep the children on their toes and engaged as others speak. Above all, this will give them an authentic experience of being a Shakespearean actor.

On first seeing Shakespeare's words written down or hearing them performed, children will imagine it being a different language altogether. Instead, focus on the parallels and familiar words to build their confidence. These are some features to focus on when reading Shakespeare's lines.

Grammar and syntax

Crystal suggests that while it may appear complex, the grammar and syntax of English – how words are arranged and ordered – has changed little since the 1600s. This explains why the language is called *early* modern rather than *medieval* and why reading

Shakespeare's lines is much easier than say, those of Chaucer. But as we have explained, Shakespeare was an expressive poet writing prose for performance. This matters. It means he was quite free to bend the rules of language to suit his purpose and is probably why his lines are so quotable. Hamlet's famous line "To be or not to be, that is the question!" dances off the tongue far easier than: 'I suppose the question is whether my life is worth anything or not?'.

When studying Shakespeare with primary children, this is an opportunity to compare how his grammatical structures and use of punctuation mirror our own. Recognising these parallels and seeing how the language has changed can help them feel more connected to his writing. It is also a chance to show that while some grammar rules are fairly standard, others are used by authors according to style and preference – quite a contrast to the National Curriculum's dogmatic take on grammatical forms.

Vocabulary

Shakespeare is famed for the range of his vocabulary. While some estimate up to 150,000 words, more realistically, he probably had about 30,000 words at his fingertips (Crystal, 2008). Sounds like a lot? It does until you consider that a 21st-century adult's vocabulary range, swelled with words of technology and science that didn't exist in 1605, is approximately 50,000 words. A 10-year-old child might have a vocabulary range of many tens of thousands of words (Trautwein and Schroeder, 2016). So, for children put off by *thee* and *thou*, remind them that Shakespeare would have been equally stumped by *pilot*, *teenager* and *computer*. This is not myth-smashing for the sake of it. It should remind us that it is not beyond even a child to read the language of Shakespeare's plays.

Rather than marvelling at the quantity of Shakespeare's vocabulary, it is his creativity with the language that is the important bit. Shakespeare is attributed to introducing (which is not quite the same as *inventing*) hundreds of new words to the English language and many, such as *excellent*, *lonely*, *assassin* and *uncomfortable*, are still in common usage. This again shows to children that the English language is a shifting sea, not a block of stone, and should encourage, not daunt, children to be bold and inventive with words.

True, his language includes technical words – a "dateless bargain", for example, is an eternal contract – and unusual, but rather beautiful regionalisms from Warwickshire such as "golden lad" for a flowering dandelion (Barber, 2015). Although many of these words are now obsolete, they are fun to speak aloud. For the teacher, this should be approached in the same way as any new or subject-specific vocabulary: taught in context and opened to discussion. Children encounter new words in texts all the time and, as teachers will know, helping children to understand them is simply part of reading. This is just the same way that complex and specific words – *digraph*, *omnivore*, *consonant*, *genetics* and so on – are taught in classrooms today and understood by teachers and children alike. Descriptive or flowery language such as 'beseech', 'jocund' or 'kill-courtesy' can be taught as synonyms for 'beg', 'cheerful' and 'loudmouth'; the meanings of other words can be learnt in context. So, learning to read Shakespeare doesn't require a totally new strategy – it's just the same as reading any other text in English.

Pronunciation and spelling

There is scant evidence about how people spoke in Shakespeare's England, so there is little agreement on how words should be pronounced. Shakespeare was (like the authors of this book) a Midlander, so he would have spoken with a regional accent and not, as some might imagine, with anything similar to **received pronunciation (RP)**.

Similar word roots and **grapheme-phoneme correlation** of early modern English and English spoken today mean that most of Shakespeare's words are relatively easy to speak aloud. The combination of sounds in words such as *do'eth, will'st, o'er* may take several attempts before children feel comfortable reading them by sight, but they are readable.

One possible obstacle to clear pronunciation of Shakespeare's words is the variations in spelling (*do*, for example, is written as *do'th, doth* and *doeth*), something that might pose a challenge to dyslexic learners. Indeed, in the six surviving signatures in William Shakespeare's handwriting, each one is spelled differently and none in the way we spell it today: *Willm Shakp, William Shaksper, Wm Shakspe, William Shakspere, Willm Shakspere* and *William Shakspeare* (Bryson, 2007).

Any difficulties children encounter in reading Shakespeare's words are likely to come from lack of confidence or unfamiliarity rather than linguistic challenge. We would advise teachers to let children read the words without interruption where possible to foreground the sound and feel of new words.

SpaG-beth: investigating Shakespeare's grammar

1. 'un-' prefixes

Common words in modern English attributed to Shakespeare's pen are adjectives or verbs prefixed with *un-*, forming an opposite or antonym. Words such as 'unkind', 'untie', 'unhand' and 'unmask' all find their first recorded usage in Shakespeare's plays. When reading, ask children to identify words prefixed with *un-* and consider what modern words could replace them. Children could also come up with their own inventions: 'undirty', to clean up; 'unthirsty oneself', to have a drink; 'unshushable', a talkative person.

2. Verbs in the present and past tense

If you read a version of the play in early modern English, explore the poetic use of verb tenses. This might include present/present tense forms such as *hath/hadst* (has/had), *doth/didst* (do/did), *art/wast* (are or be/was), *canst/canst not* (can/can't). This would be a good investigation for your working wall. Children may be able to use these verbs in their own writing to give an authentic Shakespearean feel. For more examples, see www.shakespeareswords.com.

> ### 3. Strange contractions
>
> Shakespeare often merges words, contracting them with an apostrophe for missing letters. Children might already be familiar with *'tis* for 'it is' and *'twas* for 'it was', but Shakespeare takes this to a whole new level with *in's* (in this), *i'the* (in the), *ne'er* (never) and *thou'rt* (thou art – you are). These are a poetic device. Discuss why Shakespeare might have used them. Do they change the sound, the flow or the mood of the writing?

Banter like the bard: Shakespearean insults and compliments

Insults

Shakespeare's characters were excellent at insulting one another with rather beautiful language. Many of these archaic words have now fallen out of use, but they are delicious to use and will become a staple of your drama lessons. They are also very useful for adding authenticity and spice to descriptive writing.

To generate an insult, simply choose one term from each column: Bathe thyself, thou odiferous, swag-bellied skimble-skamble!

These insults are based on those compiled by Rex Gibson in *Teaching Shakespeare* (1998).

A plague on thy house		churlish	beetle-headed	barnacle
Away I say		dankish	dizzy-eyed	bugbear
Bathe thyself		fishified	earth-vexing	clack-dish
Behold thy mirror		frothy	flap-mouthed	clotpole
Beware my sting		fusty	fly-bitten	gudgeon
Clean thine ears		goatish	guts-griping	hugger-mugger
Fie upon thee		gorbellied	idle-headed	jolt-head
Forsooth I say		impertinent	leaden-footed	knave
Get thee gone	thou . . .	loggerheaded	lily-livered	maggot-pie
Get thee hence	Macbeth, that . . .	mewling	malmsey-nosed	mammet
Grow unsightly warts		odiferous	motley-minded	miscreant
Hear me now		pribbling	onion-eyed	moldwar
Lead apes in hell		puking	pottle-deep	pigeon-egg
Mine finger in thine eye		reeky	swag-bellied	popinjay
Sorrow on thee		roguish	tickle-brained	rampallian
Swim with leeches		spleeny	toad-spotted	skimble-skamble
Thou dost intrude		thrasonical	muddy-mettled	tilly-vally
Trip on thy sword		wappened	weather-bitten	whelk
Wipe thy ugly face				

Compliments

As well as hurling insults at one another, many of Shakespeare's characters and settings call for more polite and formal language. Again, children will enjoy paying each other these rich, colourful compliments, which can be plundered by teachers and children to add to descriptive writing.

To generate a courteous compliment, simply select one term from each column: *My good lady, thou art a candied, sweet-seasoned eglantine!*

Thou . . . My good lady/lord, thou art a/an . . . Juliet is a/n . . .	airy beteeming bonny brave candied celestial choicely engilded fettled gallant mannerly palmy posied rare silken sovereign sterling sturdy tenderful worthy	best-tempered cheek-rosed crow-flowered deed-achieving eagle-sighted eye-beaming gallant-springing heaven-hued honey-tongued life-rendering nimble-pinioned proud-pied sweet-seasoned thunder-darting tiger-booted truest-mannered well-breathed young-eyed	crystal button cuckoo bud eglantine handy dandy heartling nicety minstrel pittikins plum broth primrose prizer smilet sweetmeat toast true penny tucket-sonance turtle dove wafer cake welsh cheese

Reading between the lines: understanding imagery

Helping children get the best out of Shakespeare relies on helping them navigate some complex ideas: to read between the lines and make sense of his imagery. We can do this by **taking the temperature** of the words, thinking about a character's **motivation** and unpicking **imagery** or **figurative language**.

Take this speech by Brutus in *Julius Caesar* (from an abridged text for children) as he reluctantly agrees to join the conspiracy against his friend, Caesar.

Brutus: It must be by his death. He would be crowned; how that might change his nature. Therefore think of him as a serpent's egg and kill him in the shell.

Julius Caesar, Act II, Scene 1

Julius Caesar (Garfield, 1994)

These lines are beautifully written, and as you probably found, the grammar, syntax and spelling posed no problems. We understand that Brutus is speaking and, from the context of the story, that he is talking about Caesar.

Now to make sense of it. By **taking the temperature** of the speech, we can see that Brutus uses the words "death", "crowned", "kill". Brutus is obviously talking about murder. Reading between the lines, we can ask questions about Brutus' motivation. Brutus says, "It must be by his death." Does he seem happy about what he is about to do? Would he truly want to kill Caesar, a man he calls his friend? What would he say if he really hated Caesar? We might infer that this has been a difficult decision for him, although it might tell us something about Brutus: why not just scare Caesar? Why murder? Is there no room for redemption? Maybe we could deduce that Brutus sees the world this way: black and white with no grey in between. Here the children might make links to other characters in stories or films who stick grimly to the path they have chosen even when they have doubts. They may have done this themselves.

Unpicking the wonderful image of the "serpent" in the "egg" is also interesting. What do these words imply? Why compare Caesar to snake rather than, say, a lion? Caesar was, after all, a hero of battle. Perhaps Brutus is implying that Caesar is slippery, poisonous, treacherous, dangerous. The idea of the "egg" perhaps indicates vulnerability or being fragile – Caesar doesn't see this coming. Or maybe it suggests that Brutus wants to crack him like an egg before his plan can hatch.

This is just one example, but it does show that taking the temperature of a line of dialogue can help us read between the lines to consider character motivation and figurative imagery. Just like with a poem, the lines contain images to convey the mood. Encourage children to draw on their knowledge of stories and personal experiences to make sense of them. Maybe the children know other stories that feature snakes that might help them make their decision about Brutus' words and his character. It is important always to avoid imposing meaning. Discussing them, acting them out, even drawing the imagery as a series of pictures can help children see that speculating on what writing means is both enjoyable and an important skill for reading.

Reading beyond *the lines: making meaning*

As you read a play with the children, make time to discuss their ideas on the play's overall theme. In our experience, even very young children will enjoy sharing their opinion on this. In each chapter in Part 2, we have summarised each play in one word: love, magic, revenge, ambition. You could begin by asking children if they agree with this and why. If not, what other word would they choose? Do their thoughts on this change as they learn more of the story? For example, in *The Tempest*, Prospero wants revenge on his brother, and Caliban wants revenge on Prospero. So, is the main idea of this play revenge? Or is it something else? With older children, this is a good way to discuss Shakespeare's intentions as a writer, which in turn should help them develop their own approach to writing. What did Shakespeare want us to think about afterwards? How could I achieve that in my writing?

As the children learn more of Shakespeare's plays, they can be encouraged to see connections between them. Ask open questions that will invite passionate debate. For example, how is Macbeth a better man than Julius Caesar? How is the love between Oberon and Titania stronger than that between Romeo and Juliet? This is a strong case for adopting a whole-school approach to Shakespeare.

Encouraging children to read beyond Shakespeare's lines can help them draw parallels between the plays and other stories, both print and digital, that they know. The disastrous, farcical love spell in *A Midsummer Night's Dream* might remind them of when Ron Weasley eats the chocolates laced with love potion in *Harry Potter and the Half-Blood Prince*; Romeo and Juliet's forbidden love is echoed by that of Callum and Sephy in Malorie Blackman's *Noughts and Crosses*; the abandoned Perdita from *The Winter's Tale* might remind children of Luke Skywalker or Rey from the *Star Wars* movies or Mowgli from *The Jungle Book*. Not only does this emphasise the important cultural capital gained by learning about Shakespeare, but it helps show how influential his works are in the lineage of stories that leads right to the present day.

Choosing a text

A visit to a good bookshop or an online search will reveal there is a dizzying array of Shakespeare's stories. There are original text versions lifted straight from the *First Folio*, simplified versions written in modern English, abridged versions that offer a slimmed-down version of the original. In addition, there are graphic novels, cartoons and comic strips. Where to start?!

Using a full-length, original-language version of the script will leave you with bored, frustrated children as well as very little time to do anything else! A simplified text, however, risks losing the richness and strangeness of Shakespeare's words. It might leave children scratching their heads about what all the fuss was about. Using extracts does save time, but focusing on a key scene in isolation loses the context of the larger story, making it harder to explore character development and motivation. We advise that teachers should use several versions of the story when teaching any one of Shakespeare's plays. Children will need a script to read from, a text that covers the full story arc and, for older readers, selected extracts of the original text to help them 'zoom in' to particular scenes.

- **Abridged versions of the scripts**, such as the excellent *The Animated Shakespeare* series (Heinemann), present children with an authentic Shakespearean text to perform and engage with, while making the whole story arc accessible. These are ideal for Key Stage 2 and can be adapted for younger readers.
- **Novelisations of the plays**, such as Leon Garfield's *The Shakespeare Tales* collections (Puffin), again offer rich language (as well as beautiful illustrations), but in short story format. More recent versions include Angela McAllister and Alice Lindstrom's *A Stage Full of Shakespeare Stories* (Frances Lincoln), which features most of the plays covered in this book.
- **Simplified versions** of the story, such as the *Shakespeare Stories Collection* (Orchard Books) by Andrew Matthews and Tony Ross, and the *Complete Shakespeare Series* (Usborne), offer a quick and easily understandable summary of the plot in modern English. Although there are fewer features of language to discuss in these versions, they are useful for using with Key Stage 1 children and less-confident English users to get an overview of the story.
- Plays in the **original text** are freely available online. Using extracts from these sparingly can be good for older or more confident readers to let them 'zoom in' on a particular scene and experience Shakespeare's original words. Good examples, with annotations, for those baffled by the Bard can be found at: www.sparknotes.com/shakespeare/.
- **Visual** and **multimodal versions**, such as Maisie William's excellent *Mr William Shakespeare's Plays* (2008), offer an interesting visual guide to several of Shakespeare's well-known plays (including all of the plays covered in this book) and are suitable for Key Stage 1 and 2. The *Manga Shakespeare* comics series (Self Made Hero publishers) presents Shakespeare's works in updated settings with wonderful Japanese manga

illustrations while preserving the richness of the original texts. These are more suited to upper Key Stage 2.

- **Film adaptations** and **animations** can help provide both the depth and the breadth of the stories as well as offering insights into the aesthetic and creative choices of film-makers and directors. *The Animated Shakespeare* series (Metrodome) are a little dated but are concise and suitable for younger viewers. Children's television programme adaptations such as *Cbeebies: A Midsummer Night's Dream* (2020) are good ways to share the story with younger children. Hollywood adaptations such as Baz Luhr-man's *Romeo and Juliet* (1996) should be used selectively as they may be unsuitable for primary-aged viewers, but some scenes, such as the meeting between Romeo and Juliet by the fish-tank, are beautifully cinematic. Unusual silent versions of some of the plays from the early days of cinema can be found on the website of the *British Film Institute* (BFi, https://player.bfi.org.uk/free) and, of course, YouTube.

Act I. Final thoughts

We might imagine that reading Shakespeare is a painful and thankless task with many chal-lenges for even skilled readers, let alone primary school children. By using a rich but refined version of the plays, you can introduce children to the beauty of Shakespeare's language without leaving them baffled. Resist the urge to translate for them, and instead ask them to pick up on the sound of the words, allow words to trigger ideas or feelings, and take clues from the punctuation. You're not training children to be literary scholars – you are giving them a taste of a rich and complex recipe, of a language that is poetic rather than literal. Understanding this is the key to helping them read between Shakespeare's lines. Allowing them to explore the gaps and make meaning from the words with the mind set of brave explo-ration will allow you together to read beyond Shakespeare's lines and see his importance to our cultural heritage.

Act II. Deeds: drama and creative writing

Shakespeare's words were not intended to be read silently in classrooms; they were meant to be read aloud and performed collaboratively. Drama, therefore, should be the engine driving children's creative engagement with Shakespeare, allowing opportunities to play with the relationships, dilemmas and motivations of characters before turning it into something new (Dobson and Stephenson, 2019). Drama is also invaluable for considering the importance of aesthetics, a transition from children retelling Shakespeare's stories to telling their own (Cremin and Reedy, 2015).

In this section, we will discuss forms of drama, the principles of making drama work well and basic techniques for applying them to Shakespeare's plays. Finally, we will discuss how drama can be transitioned into creative writing.

Dramatic forms

While formalised, process drama is where teachers may feel that purposeful literacy is most evident: play and spontaneous pretending have an important function in putting ideas from stories into action. In the resources in Part 2 of this book, we have tried to show that each of these forms of drama has a part to play in helping children make meaning from Shakespeare.

Process drama is a form of dramatic improvisation where participants explore story prompts, character motivation and actions. In school-based literacy, drama is positioned at an integral part of the *process* of writing, and is often guided and structured by a teacher.

Improvised drama allows unscripted, spur-of-the-moment responses to a stimulus. This is excellent for generating dialogue, exploring character reactions and getting a drama group to work together to keep an idea running. Although it won't feel very polished, improvisation can help children develop the kernel of an idea that can be refined through planning and rehearsal.

Imaginative play is where children 'pretend' together, acting out an experience that interests them, largely free of adult interference. Playing with stories like this might involve children taking on the role of characters or storytellers, or immersing themselves in a story world in role play areas, the classroom or outside. For children of all ages, this is ideal for embedding knowledge of stories as well as generating new scenarios and ideas for creative storytelling.

Dramatic principles: moving, mixing, making and belonging

Rex Gibson suggests that Shakespeare should be experienced by young learners as a fun, physically active, socially collaborative and exploratory process (Gibson, 1998). We fully endorse these principles and would consider **moving, mixing and making** (meaning, noise, decisions) as the best experiences a child can have when meeting Shakespeare for the first time; these experiences should be prioritised and used as a guide towards achieving curriculum objectives, rather than the other way around.

We would add to this the concept of '**belonging**', as we see drama as an inclusive activity where learners of all talents, confidence and needs can flourish as full participants. Drama is an excellent opportunity to develop **social uses of language** and **social cognition** (understanding the viewpoint of another), and these are skills that will benefit all children, especially those who might find this challenging, such as learners with autism spectrum disorder (ASD) (O'Sullivan, 2015). To build confidence in these areas, teachers should foreground social interaction and relationships both between the actors and the characters they are playing. As educator Jeff Blair argues, introducing Shakespeare to learners with cognitive impairments allows students to practise the acting that we all do in our everyday lives: putting on a face (Blair, 2017). With these voices largely absent from Shakespeare's plays, it seems fitting that a 21st-century approach should seek to redress that.

The teacher in role

The role of the teacher is key to making drama a fun, inclusive and productive activity (Cremin and McDonald, 2013). While some children will naturally thrive in performing in front of their classmates, for others it will be a leap of faith, and these children will take their cue from the teacher's enthusiasm and the feeling of togetherness they create in the classroom. We recognise, however, that performing in front of the children can cause teachers, especially those new to the profession, a few butterflies even with the advantage of prior preparation the night before.

Effective practice in drama requires the teacher to be flexible in their role: sometimes setting the example from the front to model vocabulary, push boundaries and steer the drama towards purposeful objectives; at other times this will involve joining in with the children as they work, or stepping aside and allowing the children freedom to experiment. This is especially important when children are playing, exploring a possible scenario through group drama or simply having fun with new characters. Drama is meant to be exploratory rather than prescribed – when children say something totally unexpected is the holy grail of a drama lesson. So, at the moment the idea occurs to you to halt an activity, restrain yourself and let things play out a little longer.

The dramatic scenario: teaching drama

The three main elements of any dramatic scenario are **people**, **place** and **predicament** (Cremin and McDonald, 2013). So, when planning drama activities for children, it is important to consider how they will explore the characters of the drama (people), show how they behave in their surroundings (setting), and giving them a problem to solve or a situation to navigate. In the following, we show how you might explore people, place and predicament with the children.

Character

Exploring characters is key to understanding a Shakespeare play. There is no narrator explaining the plot, the playwright doesn't give us character biographies, and apart from the occasional aside or soliloquy, we rarely get to see a character's inner thoughts. Almost the whole play exists in the dialogue: what they say, who they say it to, what they think aloud. The rest is open to interpretation and invites creative thinking.

To do this with children, encourage them to think like a director of a play taking into account the age of the character, their body movement, their voices and the clothes they might wear. The following questions might guide them:

1. Who am I?	• The name/age/job/role of the character • Relationships to other characters • Their class or status • Their biggest disappointment/achievement/fear/aspiration
2. What do I want?	• What they are trying to get/achieve • Who from and why • Who will help them? • What morivates them?
3. How do I behave/move?	• The words they use, the length of sentences they speak in • Their tone of voice (polite/rude) - does this change? • How often they speak and to who • Movement and body language
4. How do I dress?	• Clothes/props to suit their job/role/status - does this change? • The effect this has on other characters • Clothes and change of setting

Place

The sense of place in Shakespeare is not just about the visuals - the props or scenery on the stage - it is a way of understanding how different places or location might change the way a character behaves and speaks. For example, in a throne room or royal palace, characters might be well spoken, overly polite with formal gestures. By contrast, on the streets of old Verona, characters are likely to be rough, excitable and aggressive.

Ask the children to think about the following:

- What significance does the place have to the characters?
- Does the character belong there? Are they out of place (the fish out of water)?
- Why have the characters come together in that place?
- If it is outside, how will the weather, temperature or landscape change the way the characters dress, act and move?

Predicament

This is the problem, crisis point or critical incident around which the plot of each play turns. These are the moments when decisions are made that cannot be reversed, lines are crossed, and new paths walked - for example, Macbeth's meeting with the three witches at the start of the play, the murder of Caesar, the shipwreck in *The Tempest*. In these key scenes, it is important to consider both *what actually happens* and *what might have happened* had different choices been made. Ask your pupils to think about the following:

- What is the objective of each character in the scene?
- Where is the point of no return?
- If the decision was changed, what would it affect later in the play?

This is fertile ground for helping children to suggest Shakespeare's intentions and developing ideas for writing alternative scenes (Romeo and Juliet's wedding), developing new scripts (Macbeth apologises to Macduff and is forgiven) and developing nuanced character descriptions (what Caliban is really thinking). As explored in Chapter 2, interactive story platforms such as *Twine*, *Scratch* and *Minecraft* are ideal media for exploring these avenues.

Case study: witches on trial!

Maureen discovered a passion for Shakespeare when she was on her teaching practice. Getting the children acting was a revelation after her experience of studying Shakespeare at school, sat stiffly behind desks.

Later in her career, when teaching a Year 6 class at an inner-city primary school in Wolverhampton, she decided to introduce the children to *Macbeth*. They had never studied Shakespeare before, and, although she wondered what they would make of the language, she felt the high drama, the witches and the battles would certainly appeal to these very lively children.

Only having a short amount of time, she decided to focus on the witches. Rather than using a script, she wanted to get the children up and being active, so they started by chanting the witches' spell using call and response. *Double, double toil and trouble; Fire burn, and cauldron bubble!* Of course, there was lots of cackling and boisterous noise – that is, after all, how the children perceived witches from seeing them on television – but there was also a lot of laughter and enjoyment. This is what Shakespeare was meant to sound like!

The purpose of the drama was to reimagine the witches in a modern setting, so Maureen started to tell them a story: Some children out playing after school had seen three people collecting herbs and plants in the copse on the edge of the school field. When questioned, they said they were for herbal remedies. The children were suspicious. What if there were actual witches in the copse collecting plants for potions and gruesome spells? The children enjoyed speculating on the gender of the witches, deciding that they could be male or female. Using freeze frame and hot seating activities, the children decided these suspicious characters in the copse could definitely be witches, but they needed further evidence.

In the following lesson, the class put the witches on trial imagining creative scenarios which could provide evidence for witchy activity: strange occurrences where children turned green or grew horns. In small groups, they devised open-ended questions to interrogate the witches, tapping into their inner Poirot to hotseat the 'witches' about their activities. Of course, Year 6 found them guilty.

Watching the children work in this way, Maureen noticed how drama had piqued their interest and generated real anticipation for the lessons that would follow. Allowing the children to be so active and vocal did feel a bit risky, but it really boosted their confidence. Setting Shakespeare in the present helped the children relate to the story. Punishments for the witches, for example, did not involve water or fire, and instead children suggested they used their spells for good like doing homework or tidying messy bedrooms. Most pleasing of all, it had given the children a taste of Shakespeare that they would never forget.

Drama toolbox

If drama is new to you, there are basic conventions for helping children explore person, place and predicament. Much of these ideas owe a debt to the research of Teresa Cremin and have been adapted from a work by Roger McDonald (2017). Here we have chosen our top six. Do not feel constrained by these examples. They can be adapted and applied to every play in this book.

Freeze frame/thought tracking

A freeze frame requires children to make a *tableau* – a frozen image like a photograph – to capture a moment or feeling. This can tell a story and give insight into characters' feelings at that time, portrayed through body language and facial expressions. Thought tracking brings the frozen image to life. Prompted by an un-intrusive gesture from the teacher, such as a tap on the shoulder, a child will voice their character's inner thoughts. Alternatively, children can take turns to express their thoughts about a character. This convention is ideal for exploring group scenes where characters have different motives.

⇒ The final showdown in *The Tempest*, the murder of Julius Caesar, Mercutio's death in *Romeo and Juliet*.

Decision alley

This convention enables pupils to consider choices and dilemmas in the drama. The whole class stand in two lines to create a corridor for a child in role to slowly progress down the alley. Different choices for and against a specific dilemma faced by that character are voiced by the rest of the class.

⇒ Brutus' dilemma in *Julius Caesar*, the shepherd's choice in *The Winter's Tale*.

Hot seating

Hot seating involves a child in role being interviewed by the group. This is a good way to establish character feeling and motive and works well with decision alley to explore a character's final choice. It's useful if the class have time to prepare questions to pose to the character, but improvising this can also work well.

⇒ Lady Macbeth repents, Titania's view on Oberon, Juliet speaks from the afterlife!

Ritual or ceremony

This device is excellent for every child to celebrate significant moments in the narrative and for creating a ceremony as part of the drama. A ritual or ceremony can slow down the drama and provoke a moment of deep and memorable significance as well as a time for reflection. It could take the form of a greeting on meeting the king or queen or a repetitive chant each time the witches appear.

⇒ Perdita's return in *The Winter's Tale*, Juliet takes the 'poison', Titania and Bottom fall in love!

Creating a soundscape

Using body percussion, sound effects or simple musical instruments such as bells or tambourines can create a real sense of atmosphere. An effective soundscape can evoke an enchanted wood, a tumultuous storm or an exciting party. A soundscape can accompany a freeze frame, a narration or a role play.

⇒ Prospero's island in *The Tempest*, the enchanted forest in *A Midsummer Night's Dream*, the witches on the heath in *Macbeth*.

Role on the wall

This activity is ideal for developing understanding of character. An outline of a person is drawn (possibly around a child!) on a large sheet of paper. Words that describe the character's outer self (appearance, voice, movement, dress and the words they speak aloud) can be written down outside the shape. Emotions, feelings, thoughts, secrets – these are written inside the shape. This can be built up and added to over many lessons as the children become more familiar with the role. This activity is also useful for writing about characters, perhaps to reveal the difference between inner thoughts and the face characters present to the world.

⇒ Tybalt puts on a brave face in *Romeo and Juliet*, the shepherd in *The Winter's Tale* may face a dilemma, Banquo has growing concerns about Macbeth's behaviour.

Troubleshooting drama. What to do when . . .

A child won't participate . . . Discrete use of an adult to support a child/group can help engage them. Giving a child a camera to record others can help them feel part of things. Holding a tactile object such as a prop or taking turns with a flexi-ball can help a child feel secure enough to speak.

The children won't stop talking . . . A cue for silence is essential to keeping the drama purposeful: a jangle from a tambourine, a call/response handclapped rhythm, a quiet shush that the children echo when they hear it before falling silent. Anything is better than a raised voice. Ensure this cue is explained at the start and used throughout.

A child becomes upset . . . Give a child time away from the drama to calm down until they feel ready to re-join the session. They may be able to take on the role of 'coach' to another group if they aren't comfortable acting.

Evidencing your drama lessons . . . Take photographs throughout your drama lessons, and children can annotate with speech bubbles, reflections or captions in their books.

You are embarrassed . . . To build your own confidence, start with interactive circle games where the aim is to find a performance voice and to make each other laugh before moving on to longer activities. Co-teaching drama lessons with an experienced colleague can help calm the nerves.

Including a child with SEND . . . If a child has a physical impairment, ensure the whole group is seated so they are at the same level for eye contact, speaking and listening and interacting with facial expressions. For learners with ASD, relate the drama activities to familiar scenarios and situations, and give a clear signal (such as wearing a coloured scarf) for when you or other teachers are in and out of role. Ask the children to talk about what the experience of performing was like and where they found it difficult to participate so you can adjust for next time.

Staging drama in the classroom

Helping children to get the best out of Shakespeare requires some understanding of the style of early modern theatre (Wells, 2003). Modern theatregoers might be used to the hushed darkness, the curtain that rises and falls, the stage and backstage area – this is called the *proscenium* model of theatre. In the quiet darkness, if the play is a good one, you may not even notice the person sitting next to you or that the stage is mostly empty. This is called the suspension of disbelief. If the play is bad or the theatre is noisy, this is much harder. Plays at early modern theatres, such as Shakespeare's famous home the Globe, were performed in daylight on a stage that protruded out into the audience so the players were surrounded on three sides by the audience. This is sometimes called 'in the round'. Ignoring the audience was quite simply impossible, and, if the play was going badly, feedback would have been instant. In this way, perhaps even Shakespeare's audiences were far quicker about sharing their views than a disgruntled theatregoer blasting out a post on Twitter about a stinker of a play during the bus ride home.

For children, their experiences of watching a raucous pantomime are probably the best preparation for understanding Shakespeare's theatre. It would have been noisy, boisterous and interactive.

Setting up the classroom

An authentic rehearsal and performance space should not require a lot of resources and can be done in even the smallest of classrooms. The challenge for the teacher is encouraging children, used to the hyper-reality of the screen, to suspend their disbelief. An empty space with a chair is now a throne room; put swords in the hands of the characters, and now we are on the battlefield. Submitting to the imagination was and still is an essential part of watching live theatre.

For staging Shakespeare in the classroom, think about the following:

Space: Shakespeare's stage was surrounded by the audience, so create this performance space with a horseshoe of seats. The open space at the top of horseshoe can be for exiting and entering the space. For younger children, hold hands, take steps back until appropriate size circle is made, drop hands, and sit down. As children learn, they will quickly make the circle and either sit on floor or chairs.

Set: Set the ground-rules before you start. Children should know what the cue for silence is and what you expect in terms of their behaviour. Also, set the tone of what you hope to achieve: an objective for the lesson, that the children will take part and hopefully they will have fun.

Signal: Again, you will need a signal to the children when a performance is due to begin. A big stick firmly tapped three times on floor – a stick from teacher's garden, a broom handle or even a class window pole. You could teach children a fanfare using voices and hand movements! Whatever you choose, it is something to indicate to the children that something special is about to happen.

Support: In Shakespeare's theatre, the audience would respond to the play out loud, and this should be encouraged with the children too. Yes, they should be quiet when the performance starts, but don't insist on silence for your audience as they watch. Let them laugh, let them hiss and boo, and let them gasp. It's what Shakespeare's theatre was all about.

Speak: When the performance is over, ensure that your children have time to respond to what they have watched. How did they feel when they had to speak to the group? Which was their favourite part? How could they improve next time? Where did they find it hard/ uncomfortable to take part?

Costumes, scenery and props

Bringing drama to life in the classroom does not require elaborate props, costumes and scenery in order to help children believe in what they are seeing. While these things are an important part of live theatre, keeping the physical resources to a minimum will help encourage children to suspend their disbelief and encourage improvisation – an authentically Shakespearean way to do theatre (Egan, 2003).

For Shakespeare's company the King's Men, props and costumes would have added to the visual spectacle, but they were expensive. In the 1600s, a doublet (a jacket) for a gentlemanly or noble character could cost anything up to £3 – that is several hundreds of pounds in today's equivalent. To reduce costs, costumes were rotated between plays and actors relied on a few key outfits and accessories to signal status, ethnicity or employment to the audience. For example, a turban or colourful robe would have marked to the audience that a character was Eastern or 'exotic' (Othello or the Indian slave boy in *A Midsummer Night's Dream*). Similarly, actors used portable props such as goblets, wine bottles, manuscripts and swords to give clues about a character's role or personality. Scenery and backdrops were not used at all by Shakespeare's companies – there wasn't enough room on the stage and they could not easily be reused. Instead, other items were used to indicate place and time such as flags, chairs and candles.

These are our suggestions of costumes and props you will need for your classroom:

- A big stick . . . signals the start of the show, a wizard's staff, a stage weapon.
- A piece of fabric . . . for a cloak, a river, a night sky, to partition the stage.
- A crown . . . for a king, queen, prince, princess, or a ruler.
- A pair of fairy wings . . . for a god, a fairy, a witch.
- A jacket . . . for a soldier, an authority figure, a sailor.
- A few coloured scarves . . . help distinguish between characters.
- A plastic sword or two . . . stage weapons, a magic wand.
- A bunch of flowers . . . for a clown, a fool, a character in love.
- Safety pins . . . to attach costumes!

'By my head!'

The most famous prop, of course, was Yorick's skull for *Hamlet*. It is not clear if the first performances used a real one, although in 2008, actor David Tennant performed the title role in *Hamlet* using the skull of Polish pianist Andrè Tchaikowsky – the composer had donated it for that specific purpose (although you don't need to source a real one for your classroom drama box)!

Music and sound

Music certainly would have been part of watching a play at the Globe or other theatres in London. Instruments such as trumpets and drums, reed and string instruments were used to transport the audience to another place and time: a battle, a storm, a place of magic. In *The Tempest*, for example, music, singing and dance appear throughout the play: the sprite Ariel bewitches characters through song and Caliban speaks of the island being full of 'strange noises'. All of this added to the magical, unreal spectacle.

Music, song and dance have an important part to play in your teaching of Shakespeare. Creating soundscapes using voices, drums, tambourines and other untuned instruments can create atmosphere to use as a backdrop for a scene. Changing the tempo, volume and pitch can help control suspense to accompany performances such as during the storm in *The Tempest* (Chapter 4) or the witches' den on the heath in *Macbeth* (Chapter 8). With the help of a music teacher, some lines of dialogue might be sung or rapped rather than spoken. Using dance and movement, children can add a further dimension to their understanding of a play. Much like the way the musical *West Side Story* uses dance to interpret the gang violence of *Romeo and Juliet*, body movement could be used to explore the swordfight between Macbeth and Macduff or the chase between Antigonus and the bear in *The Winter's Tale*.

The musical instruments will you need for your drama box

These are our suggestions:
- A tambourine
- Drums or bongos
- Chime bars, chime bells, finger cymbals
- A rainstick
- Shakers, jingle bells, maracas
- Scrapers, kokiriko, guiro

Watching live performance

Children can be encouraged to appreciate the feel of live theatre by watching Shakespeare being performed live. Of course, they will get a sense of this from watching their classmates perform, but watching a play performed live by professional actors may be a new but unforgettable way to experience storytelling. Theatre companies such as the *Young Shakespeare Company* (www.youngshakespeare.org.uk) and the *Rubbish Shakespeare Company* (www.rubbishshakespearecompany.com) amongst others offer performances of Shakespeare's plays for children. Watching live theatre is a way of showing to the children how live performance offers a different experience to watching a film. As they will know from watching pantomimes, there is a sense of involvement, of realness when seeing the figures move around on stage.

Use any performance – whether by their classmates or by a theatre company – as an opportunity to discuss the aesthetics of live theatre. What did they enjoy about it? What was the funniest/scariest/most moving part of the performance and why? In what ways did it *feel* different to watching a film or television programme? What effect did the sound/music/lighting/staging have on their experience of the performance? What might the director of the play have been trying to make them feel during the show or think about afterwards? Framing these questions with an eye on the children's writing, dramatic performance and filmmaking is an important way to explore what they have learned from the experience.

An excellent way to introduce the children to critical dialogue with artists is by writing a collaborative letter of thanks to the theatre company outlining their response to the performance they have seen.

Responding to Shakespeare through creative writing

At its most effective, drama both brings stories to life and acts as a testing ground for children's creative writing – a space to problem-solve scenarios, make meaningful decisions and experience using new language in context (Wyse et al., 2013). It has been argued strongly that it can motivate children to write and determine the quality of children's writing, especially when shaping characters (Dunn, Harden and Marion, 2013). Research into child-led approaches to creative writing emphasise the importance of collaboration, purpose and enjoyment in securing engagement and in ensuring children develop their repertoire of writing skills and experiences. Involving children in this process, allowing them to make meaningful decisions about what, why and how they write (and who for) is crucial in helping children find the voice and verve of a real author (Grainger, Goouch and Lambirth, 2005).

Responding to Shakespeare's plays through writing offers the chance to explore the voices of a wide variety of characters, sensory descriptions of places, complex predicaments to weave as well as develop subject knowledge of different genres, forms and modes of writing. As we have seen, Shakespeare presents a multitude of gaps that are ideal for exploring. But framing writing for performance as a social activity with a real audience in mind is how teachers will help children get the best out of Shakespeare's plays.

Taking on roles

Perhaps the greatest impact is the fluidity of process drama which encourages children to take on different roles in the performance – actors, artistic directors, authors, audience – to explore new perspectives, and draws attention to the aesthetics of performance that can enhance children's creative writing (Edmiston, 2014). Being aware of a character's body language, inner-monologue, motivation and tone of voice can enable children to write more complex, nuanced characters. Physical characteristics manipulated, Macbeth can become a frothing 'hell hound' or a tragic figure, brave but foolish. Using drama to emphasise the speaking of language as a precursor to writing it offers the opportunity to orally rehearse dialogue, arguments and conclusions made by the characters, building confidence with new language. Indeed, most powerfully of all, drama can lay bare the process of writing, especially for screen and stage – something that can have a profound impact on how children see themselves as authors (Kucharczyk, 2018).

Aesthetics and authoring

Participating in live performance, whether formal or informal, or seeing a play performed by a professional group is to see how aesthetics – the light, the sound, the staging – can shape the shifting tone of a narrative. Similarly, seeing the plays interpreted as films, games and interactive stories also reinforces the point to children that these parts of writing are *shapeable*; for an author, they are important skills of the craft. As children read and enact, ideas can be gathered for a working wall. Notes about characters, key words and phrases, a sequence of events, an exploration of a key scene – these are all part of the process of building towards a piece of writing that is rich in creative and imaginative ideas.

Beyond the edge of the page

Exploring the 'gappiness' of Shakespeare – whether undeveloped characters or alternate endings – encourages children to draw upon their personal experiences. This might also involve children developing new stories in the story world, what we might think of as going beyond the edge of the page to explore things that might happen elsewhere on Prospero and Caliban's island or in the enchanted forest of Oberon and Titania. Digital storytelling platforms, such as *Minecraft*, that allow users to recreate and manipulate a virtual world have a role to play here too.

Remember that dramatic performance emphasises the 'social': allow children to write in pairs and groups rather than individually; treat scripts and storyboards as draft copies that should be edited and adapted as they rehearse and read. And above all, remember that this is a fun exercise that can help reconnect children with the experience of writing, especially those who may have already decided that a diet of grammar drills, cursive handwriting and punctuation targets means writing is not for them.

Writing tasks

In the teaching resources in Part 2 of this book, there are four types of writing tasks.

> **Short writing:** These shorter tasks involve children zooming in on a particular moment, dilemma or scene. These are about playfulness with language in unusual forms such as writing a rap, a recipe for friendship, a comic strip or a poster.
>
> **Long writing:** Longer-form writing tasks such as retelling a story, a longer newspaper report or a script are opportunities to bring together children's knowledge of the stories with the drama activities. In all cases, we have suggested ways in which this writing could be shared with an audience.
>
> **Freewriting:** These appear in the **incubation** stage of the resources for Key Stage 2, and they are intended to be short (15–20 minutes in total), child-led pieces where children play with ideas from the stories they have read, such as friendship, arguments and haunted castles. These are draft pieces and shouldn't be read aloud or marked. Instead, they are there to allow children to play with language like a real writer and develop ideas and words they like the feel of to use later in their compositions.
>
> **Writing for digital:** These appear in the **application** stage of the resources where children reimagine an aspect of the story for a digital platform such as *Minecraft* or *Twine*. In these tasks, children may not be 'writing' with a pencil and paper, but it is important to draw their attention to the parallels with the writing process such as building a setting, designing characters, spoken dialogue and other aesthetic devices such as music.

It is our intention that children's experience of writing should be rich and varied in terms of subject, purpose and medium. Involving children in the reading of Shakespeare should encourage teachers to feel confident to allow them to make decisions about how they respond to it through writing. Our suggestions of writing tasks in Part 2 are just that: suggestions. You may use them as described, or follow the children's interests and ideas in determining form, genre and focus.

Shakespearean grammar: Yoda sentences

The dialogue for the *Star Wars* character Jedi Master Yoda was written to make him sound wise, all-knowing and old (he was 900 years old and looked good for his age). This effect was achieved by making his speech patterns mirror those used in older texts such as Shakespeare: the subject and verb are moved to the end of the sentence. So 'She went to school' becomes 'To school, she went.'

   This can be fun to experiment with, so try writing on sentence strips, cutting it up and moving it around to achieve a similar effect.

Drama into production

While a piece of writing can often feel like the endpoint of a literacy project, it is important to show the children that writing is an essential part of media production, especially filmmaking and live performance. We have discussed digital forms of storytelling in Chapter 2.

   It has been argued that **making films** with children is not only a way of applying creative writing, but that this also represents a form of reading. The argument for production as reading recognises that children are drawn towards technical and aesthetic features such as lighting, mood and setting which can in turn help them engage more critically when reading a story (Parry, 2013). This is also true for involving children in **staging a live performance**. The arrangement of characters and props on a stage (*mise en scène*) requires reading between the lines of a text to make inference and deduction about body language, movement and how to show the relationships between characters. It also requires decision making about music, costumes and other visual clues which in turn can feed into the children's reading and writing.

Act II. Final thoughts

Drama is the engine of the creative process, turning raw ideas into fuel to drive deeper understanding of narratives as well as creative output such as writing and films. It is an inclusive activity that builds empathy and will get children talking, working and laughing together. Noise will be made, the carefully structured lesson plan might end up out of the window (partly why we don't offer them here – neither authors were particularly good at sticking to them!). But that is exactly what can make drama so exciting. If your drama lessons are slightly frayed at the edges, then it is going well: the children are thinking for themselves. Don't let anyone with a clipboard in their hand tell you otherwise. As the children turn to creating their own texts, involving children in the writing process to determine what they write and for what purpose and audience will give them an authentic experience of the writer's craft. Embracing new technologies such as film or digital platforms like *Twine* and *Minecraft* can make Shakespeare feel more tangible and relevant.

Reading

Further reading

Crystal, D. (2008) *Think on My Words: Exploring Shakespeare's Language*, Cambridge: Cambridge University Press.
Dobson, T. and Stephenson, L. (2019) '"I Think It Fits In": Using Process Drama to Promote Agentic Writing with Primary School Children,' *Literacy*, Volume 53, Issue 2 (September 2017), pp. 69–76.
McDonald, R. (2017) *The Really Useful Drama Book: Using Picturebooks to Inspire Imaginative Learning*, London: Routledge.

Online resources

www.articulateeducation.co.uk/2021/01   This blog post by **ARTiculate Education** outlines progressions in drama for KS1 and KS2 in line with the objectives of the National Curriculum.
www.rsc.org.uk/shakespeare/language   The **Royal Shakespeare Company**'s resources on language in Shakespeare's plays.
www.shakespeare.org.uk   The website of the **Shakespeare Birthplace Trust** features a range of materials to support teaching Shakespeare, including a *Shakespedia*, a collection of videos and articles about acting Shakespeare, and information about Shakespeare's life, works and family.
www.Shakespeareswords.com   An excellent online resource for exploring Shakespeare's use of language.

References

Barber, R. (2015) 'Shakespeare and Warwickshire Dialect,' *Journal of Early Modern Studies*, Issue 4, pp. 91–118 [ONLINE] Available at: www.fupress.com/bsfm-jems2016 [Accessed 1 October 2020].
Blair, J. (2017) 'Disabling Assumptions,' *English Journal*, Volume 107, Issue 2, pp. 78–80.
Bloom, A. (2016) 'Pupils Struggle to Relate to Shakespeare, Survey Finds' [ONLINE] Available at: https://www.tes.com/news/pupils-struggle-relate-shakespeare-survey-finds [Accessed 1 January 2021].
Bryson, B. (2007) *Shakespeare: The World as Stage*, London: Harper Collins.
Cremin, T. and McDonald, R. (2013) 'Drama,' in R. Jones, and D. Wyse (Eds.) *Creativity in the Primary Curriculum*, 83–97 (2nd Edition), London: Routledge.
Cremin, T. and Reedy, D. (2015) 'Creatively Engaging Writers in the Later Primary Years,' in T. Cremin (Ed.) *Teaching English Creatively: Learning to Teach in the Primary School* (2nd Edition), Abingdon: Routledge.
Dunn, J., Harden, A. and Marion, S. (2013) 'Drama and Writing: "Overcoming the Hurdle of the Blank Page",' in M. Anderson and J. Dunn (Eds.) *How Drama Activates Learning: Contemporary Research and Practice*, London: Bloomsbury.
Edmiston, B. (2014) 'Mission to Mars: Using Drama to Make a More Inclusive Classroom for Literacy Learning,' *Language Arts Urbana*, Volume 84, Issue 4 (Mar 2007), pp. 337–346.
Egan, G. (2003) 'Theatre in London,' in S. Wells and L. Cowen Orlin (Eds.) *Shakespeare: An Oxford Guide*, Oxford: Oxford University Press.
Garfield, L. (1994) *Julius Caesar Shakespeare: The Animated Tales*, London: Heinemann.
Gibson, R. (1998) *Teaching Shakespeare*, Cambridge: Cambridge University Press.
Grainger, T., Goouch, K. and Lambirth, A. (2005) *Creativity and Writing: Developing Voice and Verve in the Classroom*, London: Routledge.
Guppy, P. and Hughes, H. (1999) *The Development of Independent Reading*, Buckingham: Open University Press.

Kucharczyk, S. (2018) 'Ode to Nowhere,' *Storymakers Dialogues: Making Sense of Ourselves in the World*, Issue 1 (June) [ONLINE] Available at: http://anyflip.com/lcyg/uosj/basic [Accessed 9 July 2019].

Maguire, L. (Ed.) (2008) *How to Do Things with Shakespeare: New Approaches, New Essays*, Malden, MA: Blackwell.

O'Sullivan, C. (2015) 'Drama and Autism,' in *Encyclopaedia of Autism Spectrum Disorders*, New York: Springer.

Parry, B. (2013) *Children, Film and Literacy*, Basingstoke: Palgrave.

Powell, M. (2014) 'Kill Bill: Why We Must Take Shakespeare Out of the Classroom,' *The Guardian*, 17 March [ONLINE] Available at: www.theguardian.com/culture-professionals-network/culture-professionals-blog/2014/mar/17/kill-bill-shakespeare-classroom-theatre [Accessed 1 December 2020].

Trautwein, J. and Schroeder, S. (2016) 'How Many Words Do Children Know? A Corpus-Based Estimation of Children's Total Vocabulary Size,' *Language Testing*.

Wells, S. (2003) 'Why Study Shakespeare?,' in S. Wells and L. Cowen Orlin (Eds.) *Shakespeare: An Oxford Guide*, Oxford: Oxford University Press.

Wyse, D., Jones, R., Bradford, H. and Walport, M. A. (2013) *Teaching English, Language and Literacy* (3rd Edition), London: Routledge.

Part 2 Teaching Shakespeare

4 Year 1, *The Tempest*

The play in one word: Mystery

Although the undercurrents of this play are complex, and intended for an older audience, on the surface there is much that will be familiar to young children from traditional stories: a wizard, a magical sprite, a fantastical creature, a clown, a hidden princess and a handsome prince all vying to get a happy resolution to their problems.

On one hand, *The Tempest* is about the revenge of Prospero on his older brother for stealing his title of Duke of Milan and for sending him into island exile. On the other hand, this is also a story about natural wonders and magic (Prospero has used his time in exile to study the art of wizardry), and about cruelty: Prospero had his power removed, but he has now enslaved the sprite Ariel, the island native Caliban and, to an extent, his daughter Miranda. These are all themes that the children will enjoy thinking about.

By focusing on the storm and the magical island, this project is perfect for introducing the children to Shakespeare. With its mixture of drama, magic and humour, *The Tempest* has the feel of a boisterous pantomime. It is the perfect place to start when introducing Shakespeare to young children.

Background to *The Tempest*

The Tempest was written during an age of discovery. European sailors, pirates and adventurers were already exploring the New World. When this play was first performed in 1611, England had established permanent colonies in America and the Caribbean. Stories of encounters with exotic and strange peoples in faraway places would have fascinated 17th-century audiences as much as space travel and contact with extra-terrestrials do for us in the 21st.

By setting up Prospero as the enslaver of the island natives, Shakespeare seems to be aware that trying to 'nurture' the Other, such as Caliban, into European ways raises tricky moral questions even if he does conclude that the world's Calibans are a lost cause. This idea is worth exploring with children. Discussing together that Prospero might not be the hero and that Caliban might not be a 'monster' (we've purposefully avoided that term here) can challenge some of the assumptions the children might make when learning this story. Is Caliban really a savage, or does he just have a different way of being that requires our understanding?

The Tempest was the first play printed in the *First Folio*, the collection of Shakespeare's plays published in 1623 a few years after his death. For a long time, scholars assumed that

DOI: 10.4324/9781003023944-7

because it was printed first, it must have been an early play and therefore its themes – hope for a better world, love more powerful than magic – are evidence of Shakespeare's youthful optimism as a writer. Now it is accepted as being one of his final plays; there is much said about Prospero as a caricature of Shakespeare himself and his final speech a mature reflection about life, art and an allusion to his impending retirement from theatre. Shakespeare really can be whatever you want him to be!

The Tempest in five minutes: a summary of the play

The Tempest

Bang a stick on the floor three times and begin.

Welcome, travellers. I hope your journey to this island was a fair one. Aye, the sky is clear and bright now, but beware as this is a place of magic and mystery. The sea will not be calm, nor the sunlight warm for much longer. Do thee see that man standing on yonder rock? The man in a long cloak, blue like a rare butterfly? He is Prospero: a powerful wizard and not a man to be fooled with. Yes, he is aged, but that stick he carries is not to aid his creaking bones: 'tis a magical wand. But, look now: there is something else on the horizon. Do ye see it? A ship! A sailing ship with fluttering sails and a flag.

Prospero's eyes begin to glitter: he knoweth that flag, and he knoweth that ship. It carries his brother Alonso, who 12 years ago stole his crown as the Duke of Milan and banished him and his daughter Miranda to the island ye see before you.

Prospero raises his magical staff in the air and calls out to the skies: he commands the wind to howl, the rain to lash and the waves to crash. ⇒ **Inspiration 1.1; Illumination 4.1**

The passengers on their ship, they do cry in terror. Can you hear them? But the wizard doth not want them to drown. He wants to face them once again and seek his revenge.

Ye will recall, I said this was a magical island, and Prospero has many strange creatures to help him. One, a magical sprite called Ariel; the other is Caliban, and the island is his home. Miranda and Prospero do both look upon Caliban as a strange beast, not to be trusted. They do keep him as a servant. ⇒ **Inspiration 1.2**

Meanwhile, those bedraggled passengers stagger from the ship to the island. Alonso and his son, Prince Ferdinand, are separated and tormented by Ariel, who leads them towards Prospero's home at the centre of the island.

As the shipwrecked passengers wander through this magical island, they make a most strange discovery. A blanket in the forest! And under, a strange creature doth lie. He seems to them half man and half fish! It is Caliban, and they are most confused by his uncanny appearance. ⇒ **Incubation 2.1 and 2.2; Application 5.1 (Short writing task)** Caliban agrees to help them escape from this most mysterious place, but, in return, he desires something for himself. He wants to marry Miranda and slay cruel Prospero for making him a servant! Yes, such wicked behaviour! ⇒ **Incubation 2.3**.

Time passes, and all the passengers finally come face to face with Prospero the wizard. ⇒ **Application 5.2 (Long writing task)**. Alonso is bewildered by Prospero's magic and, afraid for his life, begs for forgiveness. Alonso returns his title and crown as Duke of Milan. Generously, Prospero accepts his apology and makes a promise to break his magic staff and give up wizardry once and for all.

Miranda, who hath not seen another living person for 12 long years, is amazed by this 'brave new world' full of wondrous people. Her eyes do rest on dashing prince Ferdinand, and they fall in love at first sight. Love, perhaps, is more powerful than magic!

Before they all leave the island, Prospero casts one final spell. To reward the winged fairy Ariel for her help, he doth set the spirit free. Foul Caliban, however, must remain his slave forever.

As the others board the ship to return to Italy, Prospero is alone thinking his thoughts out loud. He thinks that perhaps life is like a story, and the world is like a stage. As we live, we dance on the stage until it is time for us to step away and sleep forever.

Famous quotations

O brave new world, That has such people in't!
Miranda marvels at the arrival of people to the island (Act V, scene 1)

Be not afeard; the isle is full of noises, Sounds and sweet airs, that give delight, and hurt not. Ready to drop upon me
Caliban's beautiful description of his native island (Act III, scene 2)

What have we here? A man or a fish? Dead or alive? A fish. He smells like a fish, a very ancient and fish-like smell
Trinculo as he discovers Caliban asleep (Act II, scene 2)

Did you know?

- *The Tempest* is the only one of Shakespeare's plays that unfolds in real time. Rather than a story that spans weeks, months and years, *The Tempest* tells the story of three hours on the island.
- The name 'Caliban' is a close anagram of 'cannibal' and is probably used to suggest his wildness to the audience. The name 'Prospero' means prosperity – perhaps a clue that he will return to good fortune.
- It is thought that the plot of *The Tempest* may have been inspired by the wreck of an English ship near Bermuda in 1609 during a violent storm.

Teaching *The Tempest*

Summary

These activities incorporate role play, discussion, outdoor play, model making and art to act as the perfect introduction for young readers to Shakespeare's world. Further links to history, geography and science may also be explored.

If you have less time, you should focus on the discovery of the strange creature Caliban and focus on creating and describing strange fantastical beasts (Inspiration 1.2, Incubation 2.1 and 2.2) and the character description in the **short writing task** (Application 5.1).

1. Inspiration: starting with a flourish

1.1 The Tempest: role playing the storm

This topic is all about giving the children a feel of dramatic live theatre, so involving them in creating a stormy, noisy spectacle – a tempest – may imprint this play on their memory.

Gather together long strips of blue fabric (around 1 metre wide and the longer the better), percussion instruments and a wizard's cape and wand from your box of drama props. Seat the children in a horseshoe with a performance space at the front. Explain that they are going to hear a story about a wild storm at sea called *The Tempest*: they might be able to guess the meaning of this word from the word 'temper'.

Discuss what sounds and sights they might experience in a storm, and consider how musical instruments can recreate the sounds of thunder, rain, waves and wind, and how the blue fabric could be used to show a stormy sea.

Using an abridged text or the short summary from this resource, narrate the opening shipwreck scene. In role as the wizard Prospero standing on the island shore, use instructional language to command the weather and the waves: 'I, mighty Prospero, make the waves crash!' 'I, magical Prospero, call thunder from the sky!' Invite the children to add musical effects and actions as they swish the fabric. Prompt the children with questions: *How can we make the sea calm again? How can we make the waves higher?* (Figure 4.1).

Figure 4.1 Raising the storm. Recreating the tempest, as shown here in an engraving by George Romney (1797), is a memorable way to share the play with Year 1.

Invite other children to take the role of Prospero; other children could be included as sailors balancing on their 'boats' – PE benches, perhaps – in the middle of the 'sea'. To bring it all together, choose a child to narrate the whole of the story opening with the rest of the children providing the visual and sound effects.

To take this further, photograph the performance of the storm, and ask children to annotate the printed pictures with descriptive vocabulary.

1.2 Crazy creatures: creating a Caliban

One of the most interesting characters from this play to explore with Year 1 children is the island native, Caliban. The moment when two of the passengers discover Caliban under a blanket is a moment of pure pantomime that will make the children laugh: "What have we here? A *man* or a *fish*? Dead or alive? A *fish*. He smells like a *fish*, a very ancient and *fish*-like smell." They will enjoy chanting this line over and over (and over). Oh no, he doesn't; oh yes, he does! Later in this topic, you will be asking children to describe a strange creature on the island, so start by asking the children to making a model of their own fantastic beasts.

Model making can be done by making paper collages of creatures made from different animal parts: the body of a crocodile, the head of a cat, wings of a bird and so on. Cut out and arrange. These collages could be mounted on sand-coloured paper and covered with a liftable blanket for a display. If you are feeling more ambitious, your 'Calibans' could be built as junk models, covered with *papier mache* and painted.

To begin thinking deeper about Shakespeare's play, follow this up with a thought-provoking question for circle time: Shakespeare's audience would have seen Caliban as a monster, a strange and savage native from a faraway land. But is this fair? Is Caliban truly a monster, or is he just different? Prospero is obviously intelligent, but should he try to teach Caliban to be like him or leave him alone? Children have a strong sense of fairness, and this might add some depth to how they think about the characters.

2. Incubation: embedding themes and ideas

2.1 Descriptive language

Build on the model-making activity by asking children to think descriptively about the creature they have made. Photograph the collages/models and begin to build up a word bank of descriptive language. You might warm the children up by using feely bags with unusual items to inspire children to describe things imaginatively.

Encourage children to choose unusual and precise sensory language. *How would it feel to touch? How would the creature smell? Would the body part make a noise?* You might ask the children to describe the colour of the part using compound adjectives: pig-pink, blood-red, cloud-grey.

Further develop by writing descriptive sentences for each body part on paper strips: *His (or her) long, pointed head is frog-green and slimy.* Transform into short rhyming poems with nonsense sound effects:

> *His long, pointed head is green and slimy.*
> *Slippy-sloppy, slippy-sloppy, slippy-sloppy!*

It's worth remembering here that Shakespeare was a poet, and he loved playing with language, inventing and creating new words all the time. This will be a fun activity to involve the whole class.

2.2 Is it a fish or a man? Role play for the discovery of the crazy creature

Now that the children have been introduced to the story and have met some of the main characters, experiment with bringing this play to life. Focus on the scene where Caliban is discovered to help further the children's descriptive language.

Seat the children around the performance space. Place a blanket on the floor in the centre of the space.

In role as a shipwrecked sailor, remind the children of the story so far before modelling walking up to the blanket and wondering aloud what is under there. Start with some establishing phrases: "What on earth is a blanket doing in the middle of a beach?" "A blanket? In the middle of the island? Well knock me down with a feather!" You could invite some of the children up to help you. Then, creep up to the blanket and lift one of the corners. Peek underneath, give a theatrical gasp, and describe a body part that you can see using structured, repeatable language: "Feet! Big hairy feet with yellow claws. Yuck!" Repeat for the other three blanket corners, building up an image of the strange creature hiding below one body part at a time. This kind of repetitive language use offers structure for the children to base their own role plays – and later their writing – but still offers room for experimentation and new ideas. You could finish it by whipping off the blanket to reveal the complete creature below. To make the children really squeal with laughter, you could ask your TA or a classroom volunteer to dress up in a strange mishmash of clothes and hide under the blanket.

In pairs, the children could repeat the role play of their own 'discovery', perhaps aided by hiding their crazy creature (Inspiration 1.2) under a blanket and describing it. The richer the language, the better the writing will be later. Return to the performance space, and ask children to perform their 'discoveries'. The audience could have a go at drawing the creature on a whiteboard as it is described.

For added interest, this activity could be performed outside as part of a Forest School session.

2.3 Outdoor play: the enchanted isle

This activity involves imaginative outdoor play, similar to a Forest School den-building activity. It can be completed over several sessions, either in a woodland or outdoor setting, a nature garden or a playground. The theme of this topic centres around the 'enchanted isle' where the story of *The Tempest* takes place. This aspect of the work might begin by you seating the children together outside and reading them Caliban's speech about the enchanted island from Act III. They could repeat their soundscape from earlier in the topic (Inspiration 1.1) while this is being read.

These activities for imaginative play have been designed as a loose structure that can be built on as a writing task later on. But don't feel constrained by these ideas – this should be child-led as much as possible. Listen to the language the children use, photograph their work and even record the children talking about what they have done as they play – this will be useful for informing what they write. In the classroom, you could build up a wall display showing a map of the island featuring pictures of houses the children have built as well as the other features.

1   **Building creature caves.** Begin by reminding the children of the great storm, the great tempest, that they saw Prospero raise at the start of the play. When the storm hit, the island too was damaged by the wind and the rain. The caves and houses of the strange island creatures were damaged, and now they are homeless. Ask the children to go and find a suitable place for their creature to live and build a house from the natural materials they can find in the forest. If they have made junk-model fantastic beasts, put the creature in its new house to see if it is comfortable! In our experience, children have enjoyed joining these houses together to make a village. Interaction with other children at this stage often sparks the beginning of imaginative play in the world they have created.

2   **Exploring the wondrous isle.** In the following session, children should return to their village of creature caves. It is very likely that Ariel, the mischievous sprite, has turned some of their houses upside down, so they may need some repairs. For this session, encourage the children to think about some of the magical places that might exist on the island, that might be a danger or a wonder to anyone visiting. You might take them to something you have created already: a pit of poisonous snakes that can be crossed only by stepping across a log, a treacherous rainbow river to swim across, a mysterious forest. I wonder what else might be on the island? After the children have shared some ideas, allow them to break off from the group and go to build these new wonderful sights of the island. Make sure to photograph their progress and video them explaining and playing with what they have built. To finish, you might let the children take you on a tour of their sites so they can show each other how to survive on their island!

3   **Play time.** Leave unusual objects in the woods for children to discover as part of their play. These could be as simple as a brightly coloured feather (I wonder what kind of creature that has come from?), a giant footprint (I wonder what created this?), a crown from the dressing-up box (Who might this belong to?) and so on. These kinds of clues are not a direct intervention but can steer the children in imaginative new directions to generate fresh ideas to be enjoyed and to be drawn upon later.

3. Connection: cross-curricular links

Science   *The Tempest* overflows with references to the creatures that inhabit this mysterious isle; marmosets, barnacles, scamels (birds), bees, moles and perhaps crabs – all life is here; including the strange Caliban. The Year 1 science curriculum suggests that pupils explore their natural environment, so why not link the children's work on this play to learning about animals, including humans?

Year 1 science objectives (Plants and Habitats) include:

•   Identify and name a variety of common animals including fish, amphibians, reptiles, birds and mammals

- Identify and name a variety of common animals that are carnivores, herbivores and omnivores
- Describe and compare the structure of a variety of common animals (fish, amphibians, reptiles, birds and mammals, including pets)

History   Shakespeare wrote *The Tempest* at a time of great global exploration. English sailors Francis Drake and Walter Raleigh were exploring the New World as Shakespeare was writing, tales of which would have awed and inspired Londoners.

KS1 objectives for history include:

- the lives of significant individuals in the past who have contributed to national and international achievements.
- events beyond living memory that are significant nationally or globally (e.g. Christopher Columbus' voyage to the Americas)

Geography   Just as Elizabethans were exploring the world and inspiring Shakespeare to describe lands beyond Britain, so KS1 pupils should develop their knowledge of the world and their place in it.

KS1 objectives for geography include:

- use world maps, atlases and globes to identify the UK and its countries as well as the countries, continents and oceans studied at KS1

4. Illumination: responding through art

4.1 Sea Collages

For this activity, you will need papers of varied colours and textures, examples of seascapes by different artists, A4 and A3 paper, pencils, glue, black biros.

As the name suggests, this play is about a storm – both at sea and in the form of the characters' feelings of anger, revenge and love. Create a collage using pieces of paper torn rather than cut to convey the rough emotional currents running through the play. 'Found' collage materials such as colourful magazine clippings, newsprint (good for clouds) and wallpaper strips work just as effectively as new art materials.

Begin by looking at seascapes by a range of seascape artists such as Georgia O'Keefe, Hokusai and Vija Celmins. Ask the children to order them from the stormiest to the calmest – this often provokes interesting discussion. Focus on the colours used, the size of lines and how intensity is created, and think about what you may be able to smell and hear if you were in the scene. Discuss what a seascape collage linked to *The Tempest* might need to contain (e.g. clouds, rain, sky, waves, lightning), and make a list so the children can refer to it.

To develop ideas for arranging a collage, see the works of Japanese artist Yoh Nagao, Kenya's Steve Mbatia and David Hockney, and demonstrate how paper and other materials might be arranged: overlapped or mosaic style, smooth or crumpled, small or large pieces. Give the children time to practise in their art books: *How can we make a collage storm cloud, a wave, a bright sun etc.?*

Working on A3 or A4 paper in landscape/portrait format (let the children choose), show children how to sketch out a rough placement guide before they begin assembling their collage. Your teaching point here is to avoid a strip of blue at the top for the sky and a white background! They should aim to use the whole sheet of paper if they can.

In the following session, they can add other features from the story: a ship on the sea and a rock in the water upon which they can draw a silhouette in black biro of Prospero calling down the storm.

When their collage is complete, discuss how different effects have been created by the use of colour and texture. Display alongside some of the photographs of their dramatic recreation of the storm from earlier in the topic (Inspiration 1.1).

5. Application: writing

5.1 Short writing task – descriptive writing: fantastic beasts!

This is a descriptive writing task based on the scene in *The Tempest* where the mysterious creature Caliban is discovered under a blanket. It builds on tasks from earlier in the topic: the children will have designed or built fantastical creatures (Inspiration 1.2); they will have written descriptive sentences about the creature (Incubation 2.1); and they will have acted out the discovery of this creature (Incubation 2.2).

Following the drama activity, lead a shared writing activity where you model for the children how to use the example sentences they have written and the ideas generated in the drama session to compose a description of their creature.

Ensure to include an introduction similar to how you began the drama activity, marvelling about discovering the blanket and your confusion about what might be under there.

> *You'll never guess what happened to me as I was walking through the island. On the ground, in the middle of a forest I discovered . . . a blanket! A bright, red blanket. Well knock me down with a feather! I got closer and it looked like there was something underneath. I gasped. Wow! What could it be? I took a deep breath, and I lifted up one of the corners to see what it was.*

To foster decision making, discuss with the children about what order the description should go in for maximum effect on the reader – moving the paper sentence strips around that describe each body part allows this experimentation. Should it go head to toe? Or is it better to work your way up to the head? Does the creature seem even stranger if you take the body parts in a random order?

As you model, demonstrate how to take the descriptions of the body further. This might include a sense of movement, a finer detail, even a simile for more confident writers.

So:

> *His long, pointed head is green and slimy.*
> *Slippy-sloppy, slippy-sloppy, slippy-sloppy!*

Becomes . . .

> *His long, pointed head is green and slimy.*
> *It reminds me of a fat spotty frog in a pond.*
> *Slippy-sloppy, slippy-sloppy, slippy-sloppy!*

Ask the children how they might finish the story off. Perhaps by fainting on the floor and the strange creature vanishing! Or perhaps screaming and running without looking back. In our experience, this kind of wonderful silliness in writing is the perfect way to engage them, and it is exactly what Shakespeare's audience would have enjoyed. They will really look forward to getting to the last line to write something to make themselves laugh!

Give children time to edit their writing drafts. In groups, focus on making corrections and improvements to just one section of the writing. Allow them to redraft this in their writing books. You may wish to repeat the drama activity from earlier (Incubation 2.2) with the children reading out their funny descriptions.

5.2 Long writing task – a journey through the island

This activity builds on the imaginative play tasks from the Enchanted Island (Incubation 2.3) and sees the children writing a recount of a member of Alonso's crew, shipwrecked in the great tempest and making a journey across the island.

> **Read:** Ensure children are familiar with the premise of the story: Prospero the wizard creates a great storm – a tempest – that causes a ship and its passengers to be washed up on this mysterious, magical island. You could read the introduction from one of the recommended texts or the story summary at the start of this chapter to support the task.
>
> **From the text:** The journey through the island can be based on a text that is familiar to the children, but one that offers flexibility and chances to experiment. *We're Going on a Bear Hunt* is an excellent story to base their writing on (instead, it could be *We're Going on a Beast Hunt!*). Model retelling your own journey across the island using the familiar chorus to help the children piece it together (*We're going on a beast hunt;*

we're going to catch an ugly one!). Invite the children to suggest extra verses based on things they built in the woods. Write some example verses composed with the children's help on large sheets of paper for your working wall.

Plan: In small groups, ask the children to draw a story map on a large piece of paper to explain their journey. Choosing some of the wonders that they built in the imaginative play activity (Incubation 2.3), ask them to begin to plot a journey across the island. Three different parts will give a clear structure, although this is a good place to differentiate. Ask them to add words to describe sounds that can be heard at different parts of the journey – birds tweeting, squelching, splashing – or adjectives to describe their feelings, what they can see or smell. The children may wish to end their story with the discovery of the blanket covering the crazy creature in the middle of the forest. This would be a good link to the drama activities (Incubation 2.1 and 2.2) and to the **short writing task**. This, however, should be flexible, and the children may have other ideas for how to end the journey based on their imaginative play.

Ensure that the children have plenty of opportunity to talk through the story informally in groups using the descriptive language they have chosen. When the children come to write this, this descriptive language will be essential. You may wish to take this activity further and ask the children to begin using this language to write short descriptive sentences on paper strips. These can be displayed on the story map too and will be useful to slot into their writing later on.

Write: Before putting pen to paper, spend time orally rehearsing the sequence of the story. Model this for the children. Begin with an interesting opening linked to the context of the story: *After the incredible storm, I woke up on the beach with my mouth full of seawater. Yuck! I sat up and looked around slowly at the strange place I was in. It was an island! I wonder what strange creatures live here!* In our experience, getting the children to think of playful and unusual opening statements before launching into a story retelling sets the tone for the writing that will follow.

Then, using the story map created by the class, speak the story aloud, modelling descriptive and sensory language, time connectives (first, . . . then, . . . in a little while, . . . finally, . . .), sound effects and other grammar points your class are working on. Demonstrate how to transcribe these ideas into text. Their compositional focus should be on the use of sensory and descriptive language and interjections (e.g. *Ouch! Yuck! Wow! Splash!*) to make the story exciting.

Allow the children time to complete the drafts of their recount before editing these drafts in a following session. Select one scene of the story to make corrections or take further imaginatively. Once they have made changes or additions to their work, ask the children to redraft one short section on a coloured piece of paper, which can then be stuck into their books.

Share: When the recounts are completed, it is time to share them with others, perhaps in the way a shipwrecked sailor might try to send a message: a letter in a bottle. Children could copy (or type and print) their finished stories out onto tea-stained paper. Hang them to dry before rolling up and placing in wide-necked plastic bottles. Ask the children to write a tag for the bottle's neck or write their name on the bottle using a paint pen, then leave the bottles around the school for others to find with instructions to return them to your classroom once they have been found. Other teacher's desks, the main office, the school library or the visitors' room are all ideal locations.

Digital: To take the children's understanding of *The Tempest* further, they could use *Minecraft* to build a virtual interpretation of Prospero's island. This would make a collaborative and creative activity that would help children to see this as a play with a set, much as a theatre director would. Children could be given a few essentials to build to get them started – Prospero's rock, the shipwreck, Caliban's den and so on – before they use the tools of *Minecraft* to build a fantastical world with amazing features populated with characters from the story.

Inclusive learning

To differentiate . . .

- Use a writing frame with pictures to help less-confident writers prepare for the creature description. This might be practised on a story they are familiar with first, such as Julia Donaldson's *The Gruffalo*.
- Work collaboratively in a small, supported group.
- Work digitally with sentence parts and vocabulary that pupils can reorganise.

Greater depth . . .

- For a greater level of challenge for more confident writers, share some unusual Shakespearean descriptive words such as *spleeny* (angry), *goatish* (like a goat) and *lumpish* (clumsy or oddly shaped), and ask the children what they think they mean. This could form a word bank on your working wall, and children will love dropping these strange but appropriate words into their writing.
- For pupils who have a greater grasp of the story, write 'If I was . . .' sentences about different characters; e.g. "If I was Prospero, I would be kinder to Caliban and learn from him. If I was Ariel, I would rescue everyone from the storm and keep them safe."

Resources

Books to read as you teach

Matthew, A. (2002) *The Tempest*, London: Orchard.
McAllister, G. (2018) *A Stage Full of Shakespeare Stories*, London: Lincoln Children's Books.
Williams, M. (2008) *Mr William Shakespeare's Plays*, London: Walker Books.

Videos to watch as you teach

Act 1, Scene 2: The Tempest. (2017) [ONLINE] UK: The Royal Shakespeare Company [Viewed 1 January 2021] Available at: https://youtu.be/3bjrxOxIPMg
Caliban's Speech from The Tempest. (2020) [ONLINE] Kids' Poems and Stories with Michael Rosen [Viewed 1 January 2021] Available at: https://youtu.be/7cgcURLbDmk.
The Tempest. (2014) [ONLINE] UK: Shakespeare's Globe [Viewed 1 January 2021] Available at: www. shakespearesglobe.com/learn/playground/animation-videos/#the-tempest
The Tempest (Shakespeare: The Animated Tales). (2013) [DVD] Directed by Stanislav Sokolov. UK: Metrodome Distribution.

5 Year 2, *A Midsummer Night's Dream*

The play in one word: Love

Like a magical spell, *A Midsummer Night's Dream* is a Shakespearean comedy that seems to bemuse both characters and audiences alike. This a play about love in all its forms. People fall into it, out of it, trick each other for it and punish people with it.

When a group of young Athenians run away to the woods one Midsummer's day, they find themselves drawn into an enchanted world ruled by fairy royalty: King Oberon, Queen Titania and Puck, their mischievous servant. Add to the mix a group of workmen rehearsing a play in the woods and an unlucky actor, Nick Bottom – who ends up with the head of a donkey – and mayhem follows.

Studying this play with Year 2 will continue their exposure to Shakespeare and live theatrical performance. There is no pressure to study the whole play – focusing on the magical mischief of the fairies will be enough of a hook to help them enjoy the spirit of the play. With lots of funny scenes and strange characters, it is a pantomime experience that Year 2 will, yes, love.

Background to *A Midsummer Night's Dream*

A Midsummer Night's Dream was written around 1595–1596 and probably first performed in 1605. The play was set on Midsummer night, the night of the summer solstice, a cultural and spiritual event with mythical significance dating back to pagan times when some believed that transition between the human and spirit world was possible.

Shakespeare's England held onto its deep pagan roots, and fairies and sprites were a popular subject for stories. The plot of *A Midsummer Night's Dream* was likely to have been inspired by popular stories that Shakespeare would have known and read. Edmund Spencer's poem *The Faerie Queene* (1596) was written at about the same time and tells the story of legendary knights from English mythology in service of Gloriana, the Faerie Queen – very likely a tribute to Queen Elizabeth I. Geoffrey Chaucer's *The Merchant's Tale* (from *The Canterbury Tales*) depicts bickering fairy royalty, similar to Shakespeare's Oberon and Titania. Shakespeare probably also drew influence from the epic poem *Metamorphoses*, ̄ ̄ ̄ ̄n poet Ovid. This poem features a host of immoral and capricious gods and g humiliated and confused by love in the form of the mischievous deity Amo by his Latin name: Cupid. Love, fairies and crossing into spirit realms still in today. Phillip Pullman has cited this as an influence for the *His Dark Materia*

DOI: 10.4324/9⁻

sequels, where the possibility of crossing boundaries between reality and spiritual worlds is a major theme.

A Midsummer Night's Dream is set in the enchanted forest outside Athens, possibly influenced by Shakespeare's knowledge of the countryside and the nearby Forest of Arden. Shakespeare lived his adult life in the city of London, but as some have suggested, Will was a country boy at heart. He would have had detailed knowledge of things that grow, shown in poetic glory in Oberon's famous monologue spoken in Act 2, Scene 1, *I know a bank where the wild thyme blows, Where oxlips and the nodding violet grows* . . .

A Midsummer Night's Dream in five minutes: a summary of the play

---

A Midsummer Night's Dream

Begin with a fanfare, fit for royalty . . .

⇒ **Inspiration 1.1** Listen well little humans – or are ye sprites? Welcome to a world where humans and fairies live together. Gaze around you! They be close enough to touch, yet always just out of sight. To see them, ye must leave what you know behind and step into an enchanted, dreaming world. Hark! Hear ye the rustle of a leaf, the whisper of the wind – you might just hear the fairies creating mischief or squabbling amongst themselves. But, nay, do not slumber – ye must stay awake! This is a dream ye can have with your eyes wide open.

Our story begins with preparations for a wedding. The Duke of Athens, in a city in the faraway land of Greece, is to be wed to the fair lady Hippolyta, Queen of the Amazons. This is to be the finest wedding ever – or will it? Not everyone in Athens is full of the joys of Midsummer. Enter our first young couple. Hermia doth love Lysander. However, her father doth not approve of him. Yes, Lysander is most handsome, but he is not good enough to marry his daughter. Upset, Hermia runs away to meet Lysander in the forest just outside Athens. Meet our next young couple, Demetrius and the lady Helena. Hearing about Hermia's trouble, they follow her to the forest – unaware of the magical mayhem that awaits them. So now our four young people wander in the forest – and what a strange place it is! They see the trees, they see the flowers – the nodding violets, the oxlips, the wild thyme – they feel the earth beneath their sandals. But they are not alone. ⇒ **Inspiration 1.2**.

Night falls. This magical forest is home to the fairies and ruled over by King Oberon and Queen Titania and their servant Puck, a very mischievous sprite. Prepare yourselves for chaos! After all, the course of true love never did run smooth – and not smooth enough for King and Queen of the fairies, Oberon and Titania. Can you hear their furious argument? What hath raised them to such fury and anger in this moonlit place? Their war of words is so fierce that the very air seems to snap! and crackle! and pop! But it is such a silly thing that angers them – they are arguing over who should have the help of a servant boy. ⇒ **Incubation 2.3; Application 5.1 (Short writing task)**.

Green with jealousy, Oberon orders mischievous Puck to find a magical flower with which to play a trick on Titania. One drop of its juice will make Titania fall in love with the first thing she sees when she wakes from sleep. I wonder what Oberon has in mind for his wife – a frog, a monster perhaps? We shall see. ⇒ **Incubation 2.1, 2.2 and 2.4**.

As the fairy couple bicker, the ordinary workers have entered the forest to rehearse a play about love to perform at the royal wedding. One of them, a man named Nick Bottom, is wandering off into the woods. Perhaps he is looking for a quiet spot to practise his lines. But mischief is afoot! Returning with his magic flower, Puck has some naughty fun and uses the potion to give Nick Bottom the head of a donkey! *Hee haw!* Chuckling, Puck enchants Titania with the magic flower juice, and she drifts off into a deep sleep. Ye can probably guess what was to happen next. Yes, that's right! Titania waketh and falls head over heels in love with Bottom, the donkey! *Hee haw!* Having such fun, Puck uses more of the magic flower juice on the four young Athenians – Lysander and Hermia, Demetrius and Helena – who have found themselves lost in this magical place. Puck's tricks cause such a muddle, the friends awake from sleep with no idea who loves who! The enchanted forest hums with magic on this moonlit Midsummer night. ⇒ **Illumination 4.1 and 4.2; Application 5.2 (Long writing task)**.

Enough is enough; Puck has had his fun, and it is now time to restore order – Bottom only dreams he was a donkey, Hermia and Lysander fall in love, Demetrius and Helena too. Hermia's father forgives her. Oberon and Titania are reunited. All is mended. The wedding is celebrated and everyone, rich and poor, human or fairy are happy that love's true course has finally run smooth. Nick Bottom and the ordinary workmen of Athens perform their play whilst, unseen, the fairies watch from their magical kingdom.

And thou, beest thou sprite or human, hast thou listened carefully to this story of magic and love, or hast thou been daydreaming while these visions did appear?

Famous quotations

The course of true love never did run smooth.
Lysander muses on love, (Act I, Scene 1)

I know a bank where the wild thyme blows,
Where oxlips and the nodding violet grows,
Quite over-canopied with luscious woodbine,
With sweet musk-roses and with eglantine:
There sleeps Titania sometime of the night,
Lulled in these flowers with dances and delight.
Oberon's magical words (Act II, Scene 1)

You have but slumbered here,
While these visions did appear.
Mischievous Puck casts doubt on whether the play was real or not (Act V, Scene 1)

Did you know?

- On Monday, 29 September 1662, the famed diarist Samuel Pepys notes in his diary that he saw *A Midsummer Night's Dream* performed at the King's Theatre in London. He notes: "I had never seen [the play] before, nor shall ever again, for it is the most insipid ridiculous play that ever I saw in my life." He did, however, enjoy the dancing women.
- Titania's name means 'daughter of the Titans', marking her as a descendant of the elite deities of Ancient Greek mythology.
- The planet Uranus (named after one of the titans of Greek mythology) has moons named after Oberon, Titania, Puck – all characters in this play.

Teaching *A Midsummer Night's Dream*

Summary

This scheme of work will help you guide your Year 2 class through an engaging and exciting project based on Shakespeare's *A Midsummer Night's Dream*. Children will discover the enchanted forest near Athens where the play is set and meet the strange creatures who live there: Oberon and Titania, king and queen of the fairies, Puck the magical sprite and the donkey-headed Bottom. Through drama, woodland activities, model building and arts and crafts, the children will explore the theme of magic and wonder in this play. This will lead them towards designing a comic strip of the story and a written character description.

If you have less time, you can focus on the comic strip (short writing task) showing the argument between Oberon and Titania (Application, 5.1), the supporting drama activities (Incubation 2.3 and 2.4) and the art activities (Illustration 4.1 and 4.2).

1. Inspiration: starting with a flourish

1.1 A story trail: group storytelling

A Midsummer Night's Dream is a fantastical play with many strange and iconic characters, settings and scenes. Intrigue the children by casting them as detectives on a story trail. In class, set up six to eight stations each with a different story clue that links to the play. This might include:

- A pair of fairy wings
- A picture of a man with a donkey's head
- A giant picture of woodland with dried leaves and headphones playing forest sounds
- The crown of a king and queen
- A throne made of sticks
- A bottle of magic potion
- A wedding invitation

Before they start, tell them that they are going to be learning about a very old story – a strange and magical story that made people laugh, made people cry and made them say wow! If possible, do not reveal either the play title or the author – you want a completely blank slate. Allow them time to walk around and examine each clue. At each one, they should be encouraged to think about key questions, which might be posted next to each station:

- What is this object? What is it for?
- Who might it belong to?
- Who or what lives here?
- How does it fit with the other clues?
- What do you think this story is about?

Give children time to explore these in small groups – supporting adults can help them make connections between the objects and how they remind the children of other stories they might know.

After lessons like this, the children are usually buzzing with ideas and theories about the story. Back on the carpet, you could ask the children to draw story maps for the tale they imagine and compare these with other groups. These ideas would make a great display and are interesting to return to again and again, especially later in the topic. Now, they are ready to hear the first part of the story.

1.2 Into the enchanted forest: creating a soundscape

Once the children have heard the first part of the story, create a magical atmosphere to represent the setting for *A Midsummer Night's Dream*: the enchanted forest. You don't need a large performance space; use the classroom or hall space. If you have an outside space, perhaps a green space, then use it.

Explain to the class that they are going to create a soundscape to represent the sounds of a magical forest to set the scene for *A Midsummer Night's Dream*. A soundscape is where children make sounds using instruments, materials or just their own bodies to create a background of sound. It can be used to accompany a narration of the story. This can be a noisy, slightly unstructured lesson with lots of laughing and enjoyment. If that is the case, then well done for creating an authentic Shakespearean atmosphere.

Seat the children in the circle, and warm up their voices. Speaking silly sentences, changing your voices, making sound effects, using body percussion or a combination of all of these are all good warm-up activities. Begin linking the activity to the story. Think about what sounds can be used for characters in the story: the flutter of fairy wings, the wind rustling the leaves, the trees creaking and swaying, the footsteps of magical creatures. Perhaps break off into smaller groups, and ask children to think of different sounds for each and perform them as a group. Then, introduce percussion instruments such as triangles, claves, finger cymbals, castanets, tambourines, cabasas and bells. Enjoy experimenting with sounds to create different moods.

Recap on the sounds that pupils have explored in these activities, and begin to combine them to create different moods and atmospheres: such as a spooky forest, a magical forest, an angry forest and so on. Run through these as a class, and then record them to listen to later when you perform things you have written. For now, use soundscapes as an accompaniment as you read the next part of the story to the children.

2. Incubation: embedding ideas and themes

2.1. Through the forest have I gone: making woodland models

This activity will require natural materials collected from a local woodland, park or school garden, so it makes it a perfect way to combine literacy with Forest School or outdoor play. Ideally, begin by taking the children on a nature walk to collect woodland objects and natural materials.

Once they have enough materials to start with, remind the children of the story and the main characters: King Oberon, Queen Titania and Puck the mischievous sprite. This is their magical woodland, and the King and Queen must be here somewhere! Maybe the children need to use their magic and bring the characters to life? Ask the children to work in groups to create a model of either Oberon or Titania, using the natural materials they have gathered. These can be small or large, standing or flat and use any materials they like. This activity is fun at different times of year, and collecting objects in spring or autumn would give very different results! This can be extended by building a throne for them to sit on or making a cloud of fairies around them.

Support this activity by developing the vocabulary with the correct names for natural materials (holly leaves, pinecones, moss, acorns and so on) and focusing on the sensory nature of the different materials and what they might say about the character. If Oberon has a spiky crown of holly, does this mean he is a prickly character? Photograph the process and the finished model for work in the classroom.

To take this further, the children could then add labels to their model with adjectives to describe each part. This can be done outside or back in the classroom, but it is a good idea to have the materials on hand to spark their imagination.

2.2 How now, mad spirit: vocabulary and sentence development

Once the models are complete, take the vocabulary further by using it to write descriptive sentences about their character. These can be done on whiteboards or on paper sentence strips. In groups, ask each child to write a sentence about the body part. Model how to build up the sentence from just the descriptive word, perhaps using a simile.

E.g.:

> *Fluffy moss*
> *His beard is made of fluffy moss. His green beard is made of fluffy moss.*
> *Oberon's green, bushy beard is like fluffy moss that sparkles with silvery dew.*

2.3 Fairy fury: character development through drama

An iconic scene in the play is the furious argument between Oberon and Titania sparked by who will own the Indian servant. Most children will have argued which makes this an accessible route into finding their dramatic voices, tapping into real experiences. Ask questions such as, *What do we argue about? Who do we argue with? How do we make up?*

Using characters' names, model some example disagreements. Begin with something quite ordinary and show how it escalates:

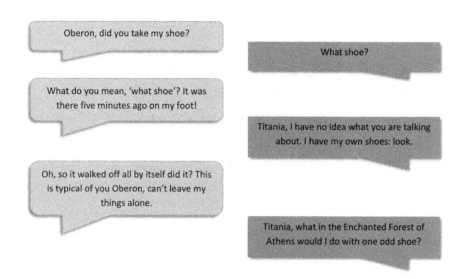

An example argument between Oberon and Titania

Keep it funny, energetic and short. Ask the children to think about the body language (pointing, sulking, gesturing) and tone of voice (hissing, shouting, mocking) as much as the words used. Discuss a phrase that you can use to end the argument ("Well, fine then!" or "Hush now! I've had enough of you Oberon!").

Once you're happy that they are able to get into – and stay in – character, then it's time to link this to the story in *A Midsummer Night's Dream*. Read the children that part of the story from an adaptation and discuss the reasons the characters have for wanting to own the boy: they are great and powerful, jealous and spoiled. They both want a servant to run around for them. Model the argument for the children: if you are confident, use some of Shakespeare's language.

Oberon: *Oh fair Titania, I should have the boy for my servant. I am the great Oberon, King of the Fairies.*
Titania: *Oh husband, you are great, but I need this servant to help me. You have Puck to help you.*

In pairs, allow the children to explore this argument. Don't worry if they wander from the example and begin to improvise away from the story; this is just to give them a feel for dramatic, comic live performance, and the more individuality, the better. You might ask the children to **perform in the round** or watch an example of this performance.

You could link this to activity 2.1 and ask the children to add speech bubbles and thought clouds to the photographs of the woodland models they made of the characters. What would Oberon be saying? What might Titania be thinking? This is further preparation for the writing tasks later on.

2.4. Fairies skip hence!: imaginative outdoor play

Transform the outdoor play area or the role-play corner into Oberon and Titania's enchanted forest. Use paper streamers, natural materials, camouflage netting, fairy lights, a fairy throne, a decorated archway and anything else you can think of to create a magical space for play or performance. This might be where you keep the dressing-up box so that children can experiment playing the characters in new, imaginative adventures. You might also make a display with some Shakespearean words, greetings or insults (see Chapter 3) so they can try them out!

3. Connection: cross-curricular links

Science   Oberon says: "I know a bank where the wild thyme blows, where oxlips and the nodding violet grows, quite over-canopied with luscious woodbine, with sweet musk-roses and with eglantine. There sleeps Titania."

Alongside the study of the play, children could germinate herbs, seeds and aromatic plants – perhaps to create their own magic herb potions as Oberon does from wildflowers.

Year 2 science objectives (Plants) include:

Pupils should be taught to:

- observe and describe how seeds and bulbs grow into mature plants
- find out and describe how plants need water, light and a suitable temperature to grow and stay healthy

Geography   The young Athenians become lost in the woods, so alongside the play children could study map skills, perhaps through orienteering, mapping their school or local area, or creating fantasy maps that would have helped the characters escape the enchanted forest.

KS1 objectives for geography (skills and fieldwork) include:

- use simple compass directions (North, South, East and West)
- use locational and directional language to describe the location of features and routes on a map

Religious education

Weddings and ceremonies

This play is bookended by weddings. It begins with preparations for Duke Theseus' marriage to Hippolyta and ends with the ceremony along with the new couples Helena and Demetrius, and Hermia and Lysander.

Alongside your scheme of work for RE, this would be an opportunity to learn about:

- Weddings and rituals celebrating love and new life in different cultures
- The significance of weddings in different religions and religious texts.

4. Illumination: responding through art

4.1. Enchanted collage frieze inspired by David Hockney

For the next two activities, you will need an image of David Hockney's *The Arrival of Spring*, for example, plain backing paper, paint brushes and sponges or rags, paints, varied textured and coloured paper, glue, pictures of fairies, straws and photographs of the children.

Try collaborative artwork to create an enchanted wood frieze inspired by David Hockney's large forest paintings, e.g. *The Arrival of Spring*.

Divide the class into groups. Using large pieces of plain backing paper, ask the children to paint or sponge a dynamic background using different shades of green paint. Make different-coloured tree trunks. Cut out large leaves and unusual petal shapes from different textured papers – use wallpaper, glossy magazines, tissue, sugar paper – and arrange everything on the background to complete the forest scene. Combine the work of each group into a longer frieze.

4.2 Designing fairy wings

Search through story books to find and draw pictures of fairies, or provide children with images of Puck depicted by artists (such as Arthur Rackham or Richard Dadd). Make fairy wings using folded paper symmetry. Marble, blow paint and block print to decorate. Create a body by using photographs of the pupils, and attach the wings. Display on the collage. Make a donkey's head to peep out of the trees.

5. Application: writing

5.1 Short writing task: comic strip: fairy fury!

Create a comic strip based on the dramatic arguments between Oberon and Titania (Incubation 2.3). This requires the use of comic strip software such as *Comic Life, Superhero Comic Book Maker* or a comic strip template in PowerPoint or Word. Of course, it can also be drawn or made with paper photographs.

Begin by looking at examples of comic strips and the different features of this text-type: panes (images), speech bubbles, thought clouds, signposts for setting and other aspects.

After making a list of comic strip features for your working wall, revisit the argument between Oberon and Titania over who owns the servant boy (Incubation 2.3). If you recorded the drama activities, let the children watch these videos again to remind themselves of the dialogue.

Start by making an idea cloud by collecting each character's arguments using sticky notes. Take further using the **role on the wall** activity (see Chapter 3) in small groups. Inside the outline, write down what each character wants: to beat Oberon in an argument, to make the slave boy belong to them and so on. Around the outline, add speech bubbles for what they might say to win the argument and thought clouds to reveal their inner feelings (which, of course, may be different to what they say).

To plan for the comic strip, try to simplify the scene into three key moments: Oberon asks for the slave boy; Titania refuses and argues back; Oberon plans to trick his wife with the love potion. Work in pairs to design the comic strip. Aim for three panes (image windows) with a speech bubble and thought cloud for each character, although children who are confident with this format may be able to do more. Teach the children how to upload photographs of their performance and sequence them in the right order. Using the tools of the software, demonstrate how to add the speech features as well as signposts to show the setting (e.g. in the woods outside Athens). Display these or bind them into a comic collection to share with other classes.

5.2 Long writing task: description of a setting – the enchanted forest

In this task, the children will write a sensory description of an enchanted forest. This activity draws on the enchanted collage frieze (Application 4.1). It also builds on the incubation activities where children built a model of one of the characters (Incubation 2.2) and developed rich vocabulary (Incubation 2.3).

Read: To begin this topic, set the context for the children with an oral storytelling rather than a reading from a book:

> *A very strange thing happened to me when I was walking through the forest. I was crunching through the leaves, leaping over logs and splashing in the mud wearing my bright blue wellies – when suddenly, the hairs stood up on the back of my neck, and I heard a shiver in the grass, a whisper in the breeze. I felt like I was being watched. I stopped, I listened, I looked. It was in a very strange part of the forest.*

To take your storytelling further, take the children through how you experience the enchanted forest using all of your senses. Perhaps using actions to help them join in:

> *I first noticed the tall trees. They were like soldiers standing still, guarding the forest. The bark was yellow, red and green like precious jewels. The branches were like spiky fingers touching the sky.*
>   *On the forest floor, I smelled/heard . . .*
>   *In the forest, I felt . . .*
>   *Behind the trees I saw . . .*

Finish by describing the 'strangest thing of all . . . ': a creature hiding in the woods. This could one of the characters in the story. Give a clue as to how you reacted to seeing this strange being in the woods. Children we have worked with have enjoyed this part the most and often enjoy showing you how they would scream in terror! This will serve as the structure to develop the children's own writing, so it is worth spending time on.

From the text: Before embarking on the long writing task, spend some time learning the short, famous poem in Act II, Scene 1, where Oberon describes the flowers that grow in the forest: "I know a bank where the wild thyme blows/Where oxlips and the nodding violet grows."

In pairs, practise reading and learning one line of the poem. In groups, perform the poem together. Listen out for rhymes - rhyming couplets. Hunt for examples of personification (nodding) and unusual adjectives (luscious, sweet, wild). Some children may be able to include the rich language from the poem in their long writing task.

Plan: Using David Hockney's painting *The Arrival of Spring*, encourage children to really look carefully at all of the details and features, maybe using magnifiers or viewfinders.

Draw their attention to three parts of the painting: the trees, the forest floor and what is behind the trees. This can form the structure for what they describe in their sensory writing. On sticky notes or on paper strips, ask the children to write down adjectives to describe different colours, sounds and sound effects, smells and tastes.

Organise the interesting vocabulary into groups for different parts of the picture.		
Trees	*Forest floor*	*Behind the trees*
nobbly orange bark	bright petals	twisted vines
whistling wind	luscious plants	puffy clouds
shivering leaves	crunchy path	curved hills
creaking branches	sweet scent	tweeting birds
swish, swash, swish!	*crunch, crunch, crunch!*	*twit twoo!*

Practise using the words by rehearsing sentences aloud with partners, adding in figurative language from the poem (e.g. sweet musk-roses, nodding violets) for an extra challenge.

Repeat the oral storytelling activity from the start to practise using the new language to describe the enchanted forest.

Write: Model the writing task, sharing with children your usual writing routines and the features of grammar your class are working on.

A curious thing happened when I was walking through the enchanted forest outside Athens. I was crunching through brown oak leaves, leaping over silver birch logs and splashing in the mud wearing my bright blue wellies – when suddenly, the hairs stood up on the back of my neck. I felt like I was being watched. I stopped, I listened, I looked.

The oak trees stood like sweet sticks of candy rock. They had smooth orange and purple bark, and the branches swayed in the breeze. Creak, crack, creak! The green and yellow leaves shivered on the branches. Brrrr!

And take the description further by looking at the next parts of the planning: the forest floor and behind the trees.

On the forest floor, there was a carpet of bright petals and luscious plants. I smelled the sweet scent of nodding oxlips and sleepy eglantines. . . .

Behind the trees I saw giant mountains and puffy clouds like smoke. . . .

Finish the storytelling with a sentence to provoke wonder and magical curiosity. You may wish to discuss as a class how the journey in the forest would end.

I thought I heard the sound of little fairy wings and little feet dancing in the leaves. I wonder what strange creatures are lurking behind these trees? I walked along the path to find out.

Perhaps you decide to stay in the forest to live with the fairies? Or maybe you are so surprised by what you saw you ran screaming and hid under the bed!

Once the drafts are complete, support the children to identify one part of their writing to edit. Redraft these sections in their books before either writing or typing them up for a display.

Share: Don't close the book on *A Midsummer Night's Dream* just yet! To get into the spirit and fun of live performance, allow the children to share their rich descriptive writing as part of a class show. Invite guests to the woods or the nature garden for a live spectacular! Seated in the round, perform the soundscape again (Inspiration 1.2), perform their dancing (see Connection), recite the poem, and read extracts from their writing aloud. Children and parents together may enjoy making models of the characters in the woods.

Digital: To take this project further, children could use a video camera or tablet to film themselves building the woodland models (Incubation 2.1). This is also an opportunity to teach them some basic camera shots such as establishing shot (to show the setting) and the close-up (a detail or face). The children could also film each other playing in the woods; this would be a fun but interactive way of documenting their work (and enjoyment) during this project.

Inclusive learning

To differentiate . . .

- Work in a small, supported group.
- Create a pool of descriptive vocabulary suggested by the group, inspired by *The Arrival of Spring*. Write sentences on whiteboards to describe different parts of the enchanted

forest. Photograph for evidence. We have found that having touchy-feely materials (such as moss, branches, leaves and so on) to hand can support their writing and help them find the right words or ideas to express.

- Use pupils' work to create a collaborative description.

Greater depth ...

- To develop, some pupils may enjoy acting out the workmen's play – *Pyramus and Thisbe.* With support, this pantomime type story can be improvised and involves a fierce lion chase, a wall, a tomb, a prickly thorn bush and a lantern. We've found that children enjoy gender swapping the roles, where Pyramus is played by a boy and Thisbe by a girl.

Resources

Books to read as you teach

Matthew, A. (2003) *A Midsummer Night's Dream,* London: Orchard Books.
McAllister, A. (2018) *A Stage Full of Shakespeare Stories,* London: Lincoln Children's Books.
Williams, M. (2008) *Mr William Shakespeare's Plays,* London: Walker Books.

Videos to watch as you teach

CBeebies a Midsummer Night's Dream. (2020) [ONLINE] UK: CBBC [Viewed 1 January 2021] Available at: www.bbc.co.uk/cbeebies/shows/a-midsummer-nights-dream
A Midsummer Night's Dream. (n.d.) [ONLINE] UK: BBC Teach [Viewed 1 January 2021] Available at www.bbc.co.uk/teach/school-radio/english-ks1-ks2-animated-series-full-versions/z4tdwty
A Midsummer Night's Dream. (2014) [ONLINE] UK: Shakespeare's Globe [Viewed 1 January 2021].

6 Year 3, *Romeo and Juliet*

The play in one word: Rivalry

References to the story of two forbidden lovers from rival families has become a cultural shorthand for true, tragic love. It has inspired many modern references: Malorie Blackman's *Noughts and Crosses* series, the classic musical *West Side Story* and the children's animated *Gnomio and Juliet*.

Set in the Italian city of Verona, the play explores the relationship between Romeo Montague and Juliet Capulet against the backdrop of their feuding families. After a chance meeting at a party, the two 'star-crossed' lovers fall for each other, marry in secret and plan to escape. Violence ensues and blood is spilled; Romeo flees for his life. The play ends tragically, finally ending the bitter family rivalry.

While this play might seem a story too bleak and violent for primary-aged children, exploring the bigger themes of friendship, rivalry, trust and the taste of first love are highly relatable.

Background to *Romeo and Juliet*

Knife crime, feuding factions and a dreadful disease: these could be news headlines in 21st-century Britain, or the plots of a TV drama. But no, these were the daily concerns of Shakespeare's London.

Romeo and Juliet was written early in Shakespeare's career and first staged around 1596. England was a divided country, and Protestants and Catholics were in conflict, a parallel with the bitter feud of the play's Montague and Capulet families. Shakespeare didn't invent this story but instead borrowed it from an English story written in 1562 by Arthur Brooke, called *The Tragicall Historye of Romeus and Juliet*. This, in turn, was inspired by the Italian novel, *Giulietta e Romeo*, written in 1530 by Luigi da Porto.

Urban violence was a problem in Elizabethan London, with daggers and rapiers worn on the streets for both fashion and self-defence. It is very likely that Shakespeare himself carried a sword as he went about the city. In the character of elegant and proud Mercutio, slain by Tybalt, Shakespeare's audiences may have recognised the contemporary playwright, Christopher Marlowe, who died in a knife fight in 1593.

In another modern parallel, Shakespeare's *Romeo and Juliet* is set against the backdrop of plague and disease. After Juliet takes the 'poison', Friar Laurence is unable to deliver a

DOI: 10.4324/9781003023944-9

vital message to Romeo because his messengers are in quarantine. Mercutio's dying curse – *A plague on both your houses!* – seems appropriate for both the play and for Shakespeare's times, where outbreaks of plague, such as in 1603, meant the shutdown of theatres and quarantine for the sick.

Romeo and Juliet in five minutes: a summary of the play

The Tragedy of Romeo and Juliet

Bang a stick on the floor three times and begin.

Never was a story of more woe, Than this of Juliet and her Romeo! With these last words of Shakespeare's play, let us begin this tragic story. Prepare ye to shed tears of sorrow.

Romeo and Juliet love each other. Their families hate each other. Why? Well, long-held arguments and rivalry can become a habit – until two young people come along and challenge the argument. Let's go back to the beginning and find out what happened.

⇒ **Inspiration 1.1 and 1.2** Behold, in the fair city of Verona, in the country of Italy, we meet a pair of star-crossed lovers called Romeo Montague and Juliet Capulet – their families are rivals.

But fie! On this day, the city is not fair, but ugly. Canst thou hear the clash of swords and vile words as the Montagues and Capulets fight in the streets? The Prince of Verona rages and threatens fearful consequences. Such fateful words are uttered – *On pain of death, all men depart.*

For a while, rivals retreat – a bit like when children misbehave in the playground and have to write a million lines, "I will not argue and fight at playtime." Will it last, dear readers? We'll see.

But here is news to gladden the heart – the Capulets will host a fabulous masked ball. ⇒ **Illumination 4.1** Romeo and his friends, Benvolio and Mercutio, sense fun to be had. They will gate crash the party. If they wear masks, then no-one will recognise a Montague, will they? Such beetle-brained biscuits!

The day of the party . . . ⇒ **Incubation 2.3** Gaze at the twinkling lights, revel in the music and excited voices, see the guests, resplendent in bright clothes and exotic masks, dancing and having fun, amongst them, Romeo and his friends. Suddenly, Romeo spots a beautiful young woman. ⇒ **Incubation 2.2** He is instantly besotted and she with him. *O, she doth teach the torches to burn bright!* **Application 5.2 (long writing task)**

Alas! Juliet is a Capulet, and she is promised to another by her family. ⇒ **Application 5.1 (short writing task)**

Later that evening, Romeo sees Juliet standing on the balcony wistfully gazing out at the stars.

"Oh Romeo, I wish you were not a Montague," she whispers. Impulsively, Romeo climbs up to the balcony and begs fair Juliet to marry him. Juliet agrees but urges

Romeo to go before her family finds him there. *Good night, good night! Parting is such sweet sorrow.*

The next day, in secret they are married by their families' friend, Friar Laurence.

Meanwhile, Mercutio and Benvolio prowl the streets of Verona. Enter Tybalt, Juliet's hot-headed cousin. Discovering that Romeo, Mercutio and Benvolio dared to gate crash the Capulet party, he is looking for a fight. Hearing the commotion, Romeo races to calm them down. You were warned peace would not last. . . . O woe! Swords are drawn, and Mercutio is fatally struck, his dying words, *A plague on both your houses!* In anger, Romeo thrusts his sword at Tybalt, who falls down dead. ⇒ **Incubation 2.1** *On pain of death all men depart!* Romeo flees to the city of Mantua for his life. Alas and alack, the happiest day of his life, in the blink of an eye, has become the worst.

Oblivious to Juliet's marriage to Romeo, the Capulets are arranging her wedding to a man she do'th not love. Friar Laurence, however, hath devised a most cunning plan. Juliet will drink a potion to make her fall into a long, deep sleep. Her family and even Romeo will think she is dead! Meanwhile, Romeo will return from Mantua to grieve for his beloved wife. Astonished when she awakes, he will whisk her away to live happily ever after. What could go wrong? Truly, a lot!

Juliet, sad to deceive her family but driven by her most powerful love for Romeo, swallows the fateful potion. Everyone mourns her 'death'. On his return from Mantua, believing her to be dead, a devastated Romeo poisons himself, collapsing stone dead at her feet. When Juliet awakes from her drugged sleep, she sees her husband dead on the ground, grabs his sword and ends her life – for real this time. Calamity.

The story of their love and secret marriage is revealed, and the Montagues and Capulets vow to end their bitter rivalry forever. But who, dear reader, is really responsible for their untimely deaths? And so, just as the story begins, it ends. . . . *For never was a story of more woe than this of Juliet and her Romeo.*

Famous quotations

O, she doth teach the torches to burn bright!
It seems she hangs upon the cheek of night
Like a rich jewel in an Ethiope's ear;

. . .

For I ne'er saw true beauty till this night.
Romeo is smitten after meeting Juliet (Act I, Scene 5).
A plague on both your houses!
As he lies dying, Mercutio curses both the Montagues and Capulets (Act III, Scene 1)
Abram: Do you bite your thumb at us, sir?
Sampson: I do bite my thumb, sir.
Abram and Sampson throw shade at each other (Act I, Scene 1)

Did you know?

- Although it is commonly believed that women were forbidden from performing on stage by law, women entertainers were not uncommon, even in the Elizabethan court. Casting young men to play the parts of women, such as Juliet, might simply reflect Shakespeare's preference.
- Romeo and Juliet's love affair redefines speed dating. In the play, less than 24 hours pass from their first meeting to their marriage and their deaths.
- The balcony at Casa di Giulietta in Verona, Italy is said to be Shakespeare's inspiration for the balcony scene where Juliet calls out to Romeo. In truth, the word 'balcony' does not appear in the play (and was not invented as a word until long after the play was written). Instead Juliet simply "appears above, at a window".
- The play's most famous line delivered by Juliet - *Romeo, Romeo, wherefore art thou Romeo?* - is often misinterpreted. *Wherefore* doesn't mean *where*, it means *why*. She is bewailing that he is a Montague, an enemy of her family.

Teaching *Romeo and Juliet*

Summary

Incorporating role play, discussion and art, these activities will help you and your class explore *Romeo and Juliet* together. By the end of the topic, the children will have responded to the themes through creative writing, art and design, technology, dance and music and be ready to stage a masked ball to showcase their work.

If you have less time, you may wish to focus on the drama tasks that explore the sword fight between Romeo and Tybalt (Incubation 2.1), responding to this through art (Illumination 4.1) and poetry (Application 5.1, short writing task).

1. Inspiration: starting with a flourish

1.1 Don't speak yet ... !: dramatic improvisation

The backdrop to this play is the rivalry between the two Verona families - the Montagues (Romeo's family) and the Capulets (Juliet's family). They swagger, they try to impress each other, and they scrap - so this is an excellent place to begin and explore the murky undercurrents of the play.

Get the class up and moving with some improvised drama. Walk around in silence without looking at each other. Then tell the children to make and hold eye contact with someone who will join their gang - they then walk around as a pair. Using only eye contact (no speech), make sure everyone else in the room knows you are their enemy! Think pulling faces. Make gestures.

As children walk, feed them information to set the scene and to provide cues for their acting. You are in Verona in Italy. It is hot in the marketplace. You are in rival gangs, the Montagues and the Capulets. As they move around, take some close-up photographs of the children's facial expressions. These will illustrate your displays and can be used as writing prompts later.

Stop and reflect. How did you feel holding eye contact? How did you behave? How did you use body language and facial expressions? Gather words and phrases on large pieces of paper to inspire writing, e.g. clenched fists, sneered, narrowed eyes. . . . Think of conjunctions and fronted adverbials you can use later.

1.2 Banter like the Bard: Shakespearean insults

Repeat the improvisation, but this time use Shakespearean language to insult and intimidate your enemies and greet your friends (see Chapter 3). Shakespeare was a master of insult, and these phrases are amongst his most witty creations that would have had his audiences hissing and laughing along. *Poisonous bunch-backed toad! The tartness of his face sours ripe grapes. There's no more faith in thee than in a stewed prune. Thou clay-brained guts, thou knotty-pated fool. You scullion! You rampallian!*

Allow your pairs to join up with a 'friendly group', and let them rove around as a four but staying in role. If they meet another group they think are friendly, they can greet the other members with low bows and sweet words: *Good morning my lady, thou airy, nimble-pinioned, plum broth.* If, however, they meet a group of rivals, they can let the insults fly. They can even think up their own words: think about the invented language of Roald Dahl. It will be noisy and uproariously funny – if so, your lesson has gone well – but it must obviously not be personal and hurtful. You know your children, so help set the boundaries and expectations.

On sentence strips, sticky notes or paper speech bubbles, let the children note down their favourites to be used later in their writing.

2. Incubation: embedding themes and ideas

2.1 Drama and sentence work: you rat-catcher!

Now that pupils have gained a basic understanding of the story, begin to explore the personalities of the main characters. This may take several lessons.

First, using a script from a language-rich adaptation, role play the scene from Act II where Romeo, Benvolio and Mercutio flee from the party only to be confronted by Tybalt. Seat the children in the round and invite a small group to perform the scene to get a feel for the words. Repeat with a fresh cast, and this time ask the audience to focus on just one character: the words they say and what this might reveal about them. *Is Tybalt being heroic here? Who is the most aggressive character? Who sounds the most nervous and why?* You might want to break into groups to let the children practise the scene.

What is the dynamic between these characters? Tybalt is out to avenge his family's dishonour (he approaches three men alone), but he is reluctant to fight anyone but Romeo. Mercutio, on the other hand, seems willing to scrap with anyone and can't understand why

Romeo won't rise to Tybalt's challenge. Romeo, initially the peacemaker, suddenly changes his mind and urges Benvolio to draw his sword when he sees Mercutio struck down by Tybalt, only for him to then to flee in panic moments later. Like any group of friends and enemies, this is complex.

In groups of four, carry out the **role on the wall** activity (see Chapter 3) for each of the characters who appears in this scene. Inside the body outline, use the script to write a list of the character's motivations. For example: *Romeo wants to avoid a fight. Protecting his friends is important to him. He is afraid of getting into trouble after killing Tybalt.* Outside of the body outline, use the description of the scene in Leon Garfield's *Shakespeare Tales* collection to list adjectives or verbs that describe the character's mannerisms. There are lots of excellent examples for Tybalt: violent, with contempt, mad, darting and so on. Finally, add a speech bubble with a key quotation from that character that reflects their outer thoughts, such as hot-headed Mercutio's zinger, "Tybalt you rat-catcher!", and a thought cloud that reflects their inner feelings during this scene. Explain how these might be opposites.

To build on this, ask the children to write a short sentence describing a character that shows their inner and outer feelings:

Benvolio stood aggressively with his blade drawn: but inside he was anxious about how violently Tybalt was behaving.

This activity will support the short writing task.

2.2 Who's that girl?: discussion point

In Act I, Scene 5, Romeo sneaks into the Capulets' masked ball. Spotting Juliet, Romeo calls over a servant to ask who she is, to which the servant replies, "I know not, sir." This small exchange might seem like a throw-away line of dialogue, but it is a strange moment worth discussing with the children. How would a servant, working for an influential family, not know the identity of the master's daughter? Is he lying, or does he really not know? What might Shakespeare be intending by this?

Most likely it is an author's technique to build up the romantic tension as Romeo forgets his infatuation with Rosalyne after setting eyes on this unknown, mysterious girl. If you're feeling confident, the **long writing task** recounting the masked ball could be written from this character's perspective. It might be interesting to think about a character who doesn't know who any of the main people are!

Taking this further, discuss with the class what thoughts might be going through Romeo's mind when he first sees Juliet. This is a good place to watch this key scene in the Royal Shakespeare Company documentary featuring Bally Gill and Karen Fishwick in the title roles, directed by Erica Whyman in 2018. The actors discuss it and then perform it. What are the thoughts going through the characters' minds? How did their faces show it? What were they hiding?

2.3 Highlights: making silent videos

For this activity, you will need a camera or a tablet for recording video. Allow several lessons.

How events in the story are seen from different perspectives is an interesting idea to explore with Year 3. Love, for example, is seen as both a moment of celebration but also a great betrayal depending on which family you belong to. In this activity, children will create a 'highlights' video to support the **long writing task**. This description will focus on the masked ball at the Capulet estate, but, equally, it could be used to look at the fight scene between Romeo and Tybalt.

After reading the description of the party either from a script or a recommended adaptation, make a list of four or five events that take place in that scene (e.g. people are dancing, Romeo and his friends arrive, Romeo spots Juliet and so on). Then in groups of four, get the children to improvise each event with *silent* acting. This removes the pressure to think of dialogue and focuses the children's attention on how the characters are standing, gestures, body language and facial expressions. Using free editing software (iMovie, Windows Movie Maker or similar), ask the children to sequence the clips they have taken into a 'highlights' video of the party, even adding credits or suitable music (such as from Prokofiev's *Romeo and Juliet* opera) to create the right mood. Watch the videos back, and discuss how they capture the mood of the scene and the relationship between the characters. These will be used to support the **long writing task** later on.

If using video clips is too challenging for the children (or for you!), ask the children to pose each scene as a **tableau** (see Chapter 3) and photograph it.

2.4 Two friends have a disagreement: freewriting task

For this task, discuss what it means to fall out with a friend. Ask what they fall out over, how they feel about it and how the friendship might be different/better after they make up. This is a story all about friends and rivals, so spending time to think about break-ups and make-ups will embed the key ideas of the play and provide inspiration for the **short and long writing tasks**.

Ask the children to spend one or two minutes jotting down any related words (adjectives, verbs, adverbs) or emotional adverbials (e.g. shaking with anger, . . . with butterflies in my tummy, . . .). Pool them on the whiteboard, and then set the children to write for 10 minutes on this idea. When finished, you do not need to ask the children to read their writing aloud. Instead, ask them to identify the most powerful sentence they have written, or the most unusual image they have created, and write this down on a sentence strip for the working wall. The ideas should be drawn upon later in the unit of work.

3. Connection: cross-curricular links

Design Technology   The masked ball where Romeo and Juliet first meet presents an opportunity to design and make masks. Children could use Venetian masks as inspiration or draw on different styles of masks from world cultures (e.g. Caribbean carnival, Benin, Native American, Chinese).

The KS2 objectives for design technology include:

- generate, develop, model and communicate their ideas through discussion, annotated sketches, cross-sectional and exploded diagrams, prototypes, pattern pieces and computer-aided design
- select from and use a wider range of tools and equipment to perform practical tasks [for example, cutting, shaping, joining and finishing], accurately
- select from and use a wider range of materials and components, including construction materials, textiles and ingredients, according to their functional properties and aesthetic qualities

Music   Prokofiev's ballet *Romeo and Juliet* interprets the events of the play, including the iconic piece of music "Dance of the Knights", made famous by the BBC television series *The Apprentice*. Listening to and discussing the mood of the music is a key part of musical appreciation, and children could be encouraged to respond to the pieces through drawing, art and dance (see the following).

The KS2 objectives for music include:

- listen with attention to detail and recall sounds with increasing aural memory
- appreciate and understand a wide range of high-quality live and recorded music drawn from different traditions and from great composers and musicians

PE (dance)   Linked to the music activities described previously, children could design dance routines or sequences of movement linked to the events of the play to Prokofiev's pieces of music from the *Romeo and Juliet* ballet. "Dance of the Knights" is grand and sweeping; "The Fight" is tense and dangerous. Watch the dancing being performed before designing dance sequences.

The KS2 objectives for music include:

- develop flexibility, strength, technique, control and balance
- perform dances using a range of movement patterns
- compare their performances with previous ones and demonstrate improvement

4. Illumination: responding through art

4.1 Here all eyes gaze on us: sketch work

For this activity, you will need images of eyes from books, magazines, simple viewfinders (make with strips of card), sketchbooks or paper, pencils, black pens, watercolour paints, cameras, Picasso images.

In old Verona, eyes are everywhere. Eyes admire and snoop, gaze with wonder and threaten – as Benvolio says to Romeo, "Here all eyes gaze on us." Combine this with the idea of masked parties where only the eyes are visible, and they take on an even more powerful significance.

In Jane Ray's illustrations for *Romeo and Juliet* (Walker Books, 2003), the eyes and faces of characters are particularly striking. Show and compare the eyes of different characters, and discuss how they convey emotion or feeling. Use (or make) simple viewfinders to focus on the eyes, or simply cut them out of copies of the images. These could be stuck into the children's sketchbooks and labelled with descriptive language. Using pencil and black ink, give children time to sketch out these images.

To take this further, ask the children to photograph each other pulling different facial expressions, paying special attention to how their eyes can convey emotion or feeling. Allow the children to choose their most striking pose. On the computer, crop the pictures down to just their eyes and enlarge to A3. Then recreate these images on large sheets of drawing paper. Sketch out in pencil, add watercolour tints to the eyes, and then accentuate with black drawing pen. This would make an excellent display that will seem to follow you around the room. . . .

5. Application: writing

5.1 Short writing task – poetry: opposites attract!

Revisit the descriptive outlines that show the inner/outer feelings of the main characters (Incubation 2.1). Take these further to write diamante poems about the characters in *Romeo and Juliet*. A diamante poem is a seven-line, non-rhyming poem written in the shape of a diamond. It follows a simple structure, with many possible variations, but is ideal for describing two complex characters. In some variations, this might be a **synonym diamante** where one character is described; an **antonym diamante** describes two opposing characters; a **cause-and-effect diamante** describes an event in one half and the aftermath in the other.

Capturing the inner/outer thoughts of characters in a word-economical poem is quite a challenge, rather like the thought required to write a haiku. It can build on the children's knowledge of grammar, and words must be chosen carefully in order to paint the perfect picture. So, as part of the planning process, encourage pupils to gather vocabulary on sticky notes, discuss choices, arrange words and play with words just as Shakespeare did to create the most dynamic impact.

The structure of a diamante poem comparing Romeo and Juliet	
Romeo	→ Noun
Handsome, youthful	→ Two adjectives
Charming, daring, fearing	→ Three verbs
Lives will change forever now	→ A five-word connection between the two
Risking, disobeying, loving	→ Three verbs
Disappointed, desperate	→ Two adjectives
Juliet	→ Noun

Begin by modelling example poems for the children, and allow them to write them in pairs to get used to the structure. More-confident writers might be able to incorporate Shakespearean language into their poem (from the script, the insults and greetings).

The most challenging line is the middle, where children have to articulate a connection between the characters. Draw on the ideas from the highlights video (Incubation 2.3) where children discussed the dynamic between the characters.

Develop this further by customising the number of words in each line and the type of sentence in each part depending on your literacy grammar focus. Could children insert similes or metaphors into both halves of the poem?

5.2 Long writing task – descriptive writing: the Capulet party!

The focus of the long writing task is the masked ball and the meeting of Romeo and Juliet. Alternatively, this task could be reimagined to look at the street fight between Romeo and Tybalt.

Here, children extend their understanding of the complexity of the characters in *Romeo and Juliet* as well as the themes of rivalry, family and friendship explored in this play. Children will draw on the drama and discussion work from earlier in this topic (Incubation 2.1, 2.2 and 2.3).

> **Discuss:** Relate the party to children's own experiences. Discuss the music, guests, food, decorations and games they would like if the party was at their house.
>
> Watch the party scene from one of the recommended screen adaptations of *Romeo and Juliet*. Watching and comparing film versions provides useful visual clues to the scene but also helps them approach this task in the way a director or an author would. *What atmosphere do I want to create? How might I make the audience feel a sense of wonder/joy/excitement? What details can be focused on to create a realistic scene?*
>
> **From the text:** Start with Leon Garfield's language-rich adaptation of *Romeo and Juliet* from his classic collection of *Shakespeare Stories* where Romeo and his Montague friends gather outside the Capulet mansion in fancy dress, ready to sneak in to the party (Garfield, 1985, p. 207). Remind yourselves why they are there: to cause mischief, have fun and help Romeo forget his former friend, Rosalyne.
>
> As the children read, ask them to pick out their favourite descriptions of the party, such as "bubbling laughter as a glass of good wine" or how the guests in their costumes are as "gorgeous dragonflies, with partly folded wings".
>
> Building on the party plan, write a short sensory paragraph describing the scene. Aim for around five or six sentences using descriptive and figurative language.

> *In a corner, a group of children giggled and fizzed like bubbling cola bottles. The ladies wore bright salwar kameezes of pinks and golds that shimmered like butterfly wings. The air was filled with fragrant smells, and guests munched on samosas and sticky sweets. Old men sat and rested their bones. Young couples danced and looked at each other with love in their eyes.*

Plan: Revisit the highlights video the children made earlier showing the events at the ball (Incubation 2.3). This resource will remind them of the sequence of events and give them emotions, actions and atmosphere to describe.

Decide whose point of view the recount will be told from: will it be Romeo? Will it be Tybalt? Could you imagine yourself at the party? How about a complete stranger? (Incubation 2.2).

As they watch the highlights video, ask the children to work in pairs to write a sentence for each clip or still. Start simple and just describe the action: *The music started and everyone began to dance, but Romeo was not enjoying himself*. Then model how to develop each, orally incorporating ideas you have discussed:

> *The band started to play a lively song, and everyone jumped onto the dance floor. Dresses swayed to the rhythm like tropical flowers. From everywhere there was singing and laughter like the pop of champagne corks. But, on the other side of the dance floor, one young man stood like a storm cloud. I think his name was Romeo. Whoever he was, he was not having a good time.*

Let the children rehearse telling the story orally to a partner or a group, building up the complexity of their ideas. To follow up, they might write down their favourite idea onto sentence strips and add it to the writing wall.

Write: The writing task will be to retell the events of the Capulet feast from the point of view of someone who was there. Allowing children to decide who this will be and to draw on their personal experiences of what makes a good family party is where the creative thinking comes into this task. As well as retelling the events, a good recount should include a setting description, character, action and dialogue. Show the children how to use their party descriptions to write an introduction to the writing. Take it further by describing the characters who are there and the events that take place. For an extra challenge, you could ask them to imagine a different ending to the scene, one where Romeo and Tybalt are reconciled and the division between the families is healed. Discuss with the children how they might avoid the violent and tragic events that are set to follow.

Allow the children time to edit their writing with a focus on making corrections and improvements to two sections: the party scene and an area of their story they feel needs developing.

Share: Holding a masked ball would be an excellent way to bring this topic to a close. Wearing their party clothes and Venetian masks, the children could stage an Italian style *passeggiata*, the traditional slow stroll through the main streets of the city, showing off their finery and their companions. You could even repeat the Shakespearean language game (Inspiration 1.2) and greet your friends sweetly while insulting your enemies using the Bard's barbed words. Once they have warmed up, seat the children in the round and have them take turns stepping into the centre to read aloud part of their recount. It will be a fantastic opportunity to hear their beautiful descriptions and feisty action from the party. Once the work is done, give them chance to strut their stuff, eat party snacks and play games. A wonderful way to end the unit of work.

Digital: A fun way to bring in digital storytelling would be to reimagine the classic *Scratch* animation project *Dance Party* as the Capulet ball from *Romeo and Juliet*. This is an ideal project if you are just getting started with *Scratch* animation, as the pre-existing code can be easily edited and customised. Children can photograph themselves in costume in a variety of dance poses to use as new sprites; the background and the music can also be changed. For an extra challenge, children could include speech and quotations from the play, or turn it into a game where players have to copy particular dance moves to complete a level. It is ideal as an open-ended creative challenge! The original (and dangerously catchy) *Dance Party* animation can be found at: https://scratch.mit.edu/projects/10128067

Inclusive learning

To differentiate . . .

- For EAL or lower reading abilities, consider simplifying the text, but take care to retain some of the original richness of the language.
- Ask pupils to pose for a series of photographs showing scenes at the party. Work digitally or print them out to create thought bubbles and speech bubbles to express the narrative. This will not only support pupils in structuring their writing but will embed the idea that characters in stories can think one thing but say another.

Greater depth . . .

- To take the long writing task further, ask more confident readers to work with an extract from the original play to look for descriptive clues. Encourage pupils to incorporate Shakespearean phrases from the story into their writing. *Thou villain Capulet! They'll make worms meat of me!*

Resources

Books to read as you teach

Garfield, L. (1985) *Shakespeare Stories*, London: Victor Gollancz.
McAllister, A. (2018) *A Stage Full of Shakespeare Stories*, London: Lincoln Children's Books.
Plaisted, C. A. (2012) *Tales from Shakespeare, Romeo and Juliet, Retold in Modern-Day English*, London: QED Publishing.
Powel, M. (2012) *Shakespeare's Romeo and Juliet*, London: Raintree.
Rosen, M. and Ray, J. (2003) *Shakespeare's Romeo and Juliet*, London: Walker Books.

Videos to watch as you teach

Romeo and Juliet. (2014) [ONLINE] UK: Shakespeare's Globe [Viewed 1 January 2021] Available at: www.shakespearesglobe.com/learn/playground/animation-videos/#romeo-juliet
Romeo and Juliet, Act 1 Scene 5. (2018) [ONLINE] UK: Royal Shakespeare Company [Viewed 1 January 2021] Available at: www.youtube.com/watch?v=gl5Sz2oZco8
Roseo and Julius. (2015) [ONLINE] UK: ARTiculate Education Available at: www.articulateeducation.co.uk/p/gallery.html

7 Year 4, *Julius Caesar*

The play in one word: Ambition

Julius Caesar is both a political drama and a tragedy exploring the events surrounding the murder of this famous Roman general. Fresh from military conquest, Caesar's reputation is on the rise, with the Roman mob calling for him to be made king and end the representative rule of the Senate. Alarmed by what Caesar's rise might mean for the future of the Roman Republic, a group of senators (and some of Caesar's closest allies) conspire to murder him. While the murder unusually comes in the middle of the story (rather than at the climax), the final stages show the conspirators and Caesar's loyal friends managing the fallout of the murder, notably with speeches appealing to the fickle friends, Romans and countrymen of the Roman public.

Julius Caesar is a play about ambition and power, friendship and betrayal. The theme of regicide (killing a monarch) appears again and again in Shakespeare's plays (*Macbeth*, *King Lear*, *Hamlet* and more), and the idea of a despot on the rise and the hard choices facing those who resist appears in stories such as the *Lion King* and *Star Wars*.

Studying this play with children is an opportunity to explore persuasive writing and consider themes such as fairness and decision making. There are lots of pathways into other areas of the curriculum other than history, especially ideas around government and representation, which support PSHE and citizenship.

Background to *Julius Caesar*

Writing a play in England in the late 1500s was a risky business, especially if your plot strayed into the territory of political satire. The 'Bishop's Ban' of 1599 tightened state censorship rules, so it is possible that, in order to steer clear of trouble, Shakespeare deliberately opted to write about a figure from antiquity to make his point about the dangers of absolute power.

That is not to say that the themes of *Julius Caesar* did not push contemporary buttons for his audience. The murder of a ruler would have been a serious concern for the men and women of England, and Elizabeth I lived in paranoid fear of political assassination by her enemies. Early modern England was a time when transition between monarchs was rarely peaceful and the succession to childless Elizabeth - Caesar was also without a designated heir - may have led to violent upheaval, even civil war. It was perhaps why regicide - the murder of a monarch - was a theme that Shakespeare returned to throughout his career.

DOI: 10.4324/9781003023944-10

Julius Caesar was probably first performed in September 1599 to launch the newly opened Globe Theatre. This can be guessed at because of an entry in the diary of a Swiss tourist to London named Thomas Platter, who saw it performed that month at the Globe, noting that it was "pleasingly performed" by a cast of 15 actors. Platter also notes that the conclusion of the play, slightly incongruously, was followed by lots of marvellous dancing by the cast. Hail Caesar!

Julius Caesar *in five minutes: a summary of the play*

The tragedy of Julius Caesar

Bang a drum three times. Hurrah! Hurrah! Hurrah!

Hail Caesar! Citizens. Can ye see this noble, powerful general marching triumphantly into the ancient city of Rome? It is the year 44 bc. The terracotta rooftops shine in the early March sunshine. Below, the streets throng and resound with Roman cheers. They cheer for Julius Caesar, Rome's victorious hero. Hurrah, hail Caesar!

Citizens, cease your cheering for a moment. Rome is governed democratically by the Senate. Caesar is an ambitious man - his return may well destroy the peace. Secretly, the senators, men like Brutus, Casca, Cinna and Cassius, fear that Caesar may become emperor of Rome, and they fear for their own power. ⇒ **Inspiration 1.1**

To the streets of Rome, we return. . . . Hail Caesar! An old man, a soothsayer pushes through the cheering throngs. "Beware the Ides of March!" he hisses at Caesar. Such superstitious foolishness - Caesar pushes him away. Hail Caesar! ⇒ **Inspiration 1.2**

'Tis night, and a violent storm does rage over Rome, and the Senators brood over their most secret thoughts. Casca, Cinna and Cassius implore good Brutus to act; but Brutus is an honourable man, and his thoughts are as tumultuous as the storm. Can ye smell their conspiracy, citizens? A plot is afoot. . . . Caesar must die before he can become emperor and destroy their power: they must crush the serpent's egg before it hatches. ⇒ **Incubation 2.2 and 2.3**.

Morning dawns. Beware the Ides of March - the 15th day of March is upon us! As Caesar enters the Senate building to discuss the business of the day, Brutus and the others encircle Caesar, and he is slain by bloody, treacherous daggers. Brutus strikes the final, fatal cut - Et tu, Brute? ⇒ **Incubation 2.1**

In Rome, those who cheered for Caesar's return, they do now bray most fiercely for justice. Outside Rome, news of Caesar's brutal end reaches his friend and ally Mark Antony, who races to the city to seek revenge.

Outside the Senate, Brutus speaketh in front of the angry crowd. His sweet words do persuade them that Caesar's death was just; his power *was* to be feared. Can ye hear their roar of approval? Yet when Mark Antony addresses the crowd, his words do show Caesar's death is to be mourned as a great loss to Rome. ⇒ **Illumination 4.1** Lend me your ears! O, fickle crowd. They turn on the Senators and kill them! ⇒ **Incubation 2.4** In the chaos, Brutus and Cassius flee for their lives. A bloodthirsty battle rages, and Cassius and Brutus die in shame for their part in Caesar's downfall.

Aye Citizens, Mark Antony prevails, and his most feared ally, Octavius, is crowned emperor of Rome. Hail Octavius! ⇒**Application 5.1 and 5.2 (short and long writing tasks)** And so this bloodthirsty tale of power and ambition doth end.

Famous quotations

Et tu, Brute?
Caesar's dying words to his friend Brutus, now an accomplice to his murder (Act III, Scene 1)
Friends, Romans, countrymen, lend me your ears.
I have come to bury Caesar, not to praise him.
The evil that men do lives after them;
The good is oft interred with their bones.
Mark Antony's eloquent speech at Caesar's funeral (Act III, Scene 2)
Beware the Ides of March!
Caesar is warned of impending doom by a soothsayer (Act I, Scene 1)

Did you know?

- Julius Caesar was the first Roman politician to have his own portrait minted on a coin during his lifetime.
- Over 60 people were involved in Caesar's assassination. This prevented any one individual from taking the blame.
- Together with the astronomer Sosognes in 45 bc, Caesar designed a calendar to include a leap year. We call this the Julian Calendar, and it was in use in Britain until the 1580s. It was still in use in Russia until 1917.
- Mark Antony also features in Shakespeare's play *Antony and Cleopatra*, performed in 1607. He is only one of a handful of characters to appear in more than one Shakespeare play.

Teaching *Julius Caesar*

Summary

Julius Caesar is a bloodthirsty play with ambition, power, betrayal, friendship and politics at its heart. It is an excellent opportunity to study choices and consequences with KS2 as well as links with the wider curriculum, incorporating drama, art, history, RE and PSHE. The activities have been designed to lead your class towards a dramatic re-enactment of the grand speeches by Brutus and Mark Antony on the steps of the Senate.

If you have less time, you can focus on the scene where Julius Caesar is assassinated. Activities 2.1, 2.2 and 2.3 focus on the character of Caesar and the reasons for his murder before preparing election posters to rival his power (Application 5.1, short writing task).

1. Inspiration: starting with a flourish

1.1 Decisions, decisions: a game to explore the nature of leadership

The story of *Julius Caesar* is positioned at a defining moment in the history of the ancient Romans: the transition from a republic to a dictatorship. As a successful military general return-ing from conquest, Caesar is motivated to impose his will on the government and place himself in charge. Understanding this is key to understanding both his motives and why he is murdered.

An effective way to convey this to the children is through games. Split the class into two teams. Team A cannot communicate with each other and have to take direct instructions from just one nominated person (the dictator); the Team B have to decide as a group upon their actions before acting (a council or, as the Romans called it, the Senate).

Give both teams a series of identical tasks to complete against the clock: completing a jigsaw puzzle, passing a ball through an obstacle course, retelling a story one word at a time and so on. But at all times, Team A must act only as the dictator tells them to, while Team B can discuss and find agreement as they go along. When they have completed some of the tasks, pose questions to the children: *Which team made decisions the fastest? Which team made the best choices? If the team fails, who is responsible? How did you feel about not having your chance to decide?*

Discussing leadership is central to understanding the plot of *Julius Caesar* and the motiva-tion of the main character. The ideas these discussions generate will form the context for the unit of work that follows.

1.2 Beware the ides of March! A class discussion about superstition

At the very start of the play, Caesar walks down the steps of the Senate building in Rome and is approached by a soothsayer: a fortune teller. The man warns Caesar of impending doom on the Ides of March (15 March and an inauspicious day). Caesar ignores it, laughing it off as superstition, but as often happens with Shakespeare's characters, ignoring the warning signs is usually a bad idea. Just ask Macbeth.

As a class, discuss the nature of superstitions, and ask the children to share examples from their family (tossing salt over your shoulder, not walking under ladders, not stepping on three drain covers in a row). You might also discuss examples of superstition of sportspeople and athletes to bring them luck before a game or race. Serena Williams, for example, has to tie her shoelaces in exactly the same way before every tennis match.

Bringing it back to the play, think whether it would have helped Caesar to be more supersti-tious or less. If he had listened to the soothsayer, might this all have been avoided? Or was his death inevitable? You might also ask the children to research ancient Roman superstitions and bad omens. There are lots of them, including some very familiar ones: the idea of getting out of bed on the 'right side' might have been a Roman tradition, as the left side was considered unlucky.

2. Incubation: embedding themes and ideas

2.1 Friends and Romans: role playing the murder of Julius Caesar

It is a curious feature of this play that the characters who stand for representative, fairer government – Brutus and Cassius – are cast as the story's villains. The dictator Caesar and his chief supporter, Mark Antony, are cast as the martyr and the hero. Perhaps this is reflective of Shakespeare's unwillingness to fall foul of censorship laws by portraying royal rule as an oppressive evil.

The murder of Caesar is the pivot of the whole story. If time is short, this is the scene to focus on. With the children, role play the assassination using a simple script (see Leon Garfield's abridged version in the recommended reading list). Seat the whole class in the round, assign children to act the parts of Caesar and the conspirators, and role play the scene. Once this has been run through, ask the children the following:

- Is this a crime or an 'honourable' act?
- What are the motives of these men to kill Caesar?
- How could they justify their actions?

Discuss possible motives for the characters, and gather ideas in a Venn Diagram: honourable motives, wicked motives, and the ones that overlap.

Back to the drama. If the senators are villains, then this will impact their body language, their tone of voice and the way they move. Similarly, if Caesar is the noble victim or a slain tyrant, this will impact how he speaks, gestures and moves. Rotate the cast and role play again, this time making conscious choices to show the senators as villains. Ask the children to speak aloud an improvised line of dialogue to explain a motive for their character before they stick the knife (or ruler) into Caesar. Repeat, but this time playing it as a heroic act with noble motives spoken aloud. *Which is the most believable performance?*

To take further, organise the children into groups of six and ask them to make a directorial decision about how they will represent the scene. Allow time to rehearse and to practise speaking their improvised lines to explain the characters' motives. Photograph the children as they rehearse (useful for writing later) before coming together to perform their take on the scene. Discuss any similarities or differences with how the scenes are performed.

2.2 Hearts and minds: character and vocabulary development

To support the writing and drama tasks, it is important to understand the characters and their motivations, as well as having a bank of descriptive language to describe each character. This activity should be done with either an accompanying copy of the abridged script or after watching or reading a particular version of the story. In our experience, this kind of activity not only deepens the children's understanding of a play but also is a foundation for expressive creative writing that is authentic.

To start, provide the children with an image of the plotters in Brutus' orchard. There are many fine examples to be found online of Victorian engravings depicting the scene as well as modern versions from the Royal Shakespeare Company. Of course, it would also be good to ask the children to freeze frame the scene depicting Brutus, Cassius, Casca, Cinna and the others who appear in Act II, Scene 1 and photograph it.

Using the script or supported by a chosen version of the story, read through the scene where the plotters make their case for killing Caesar to a reluctant Brutus. Based on the dialogue, ask the children to identify in the image who the different characters might be from their body language and facial expressions; they can draw the names on the photograph. It doesn't matter if they don't come to a class consensus about who's who – it is their reasoning that has value here. Drawing from the story, ask the children to identify the **hearts and minds** – the inner and outer thoughts – of each character. You might relate this to the two-faced Roman god, Janus, who looks one way and the other, suggesting that he might not be completely honest.

For the mind, draw on a speech bubble for each character giving a reason why they wish to kill Caesar. For example, Brutus might say: "It must be by his death. How much would the crown change him?" Then to the hearts – what is each character feeling about this decision? Brutus is certainly in conflict, so is his heart saying something different? Cassius, for example, is deeply envious of Caesar's popularity, so his inner thoughts might reflect this: "You don't deserve such popularity, Caesar. I am a greater man than you!" Once complete, the children could return to the freeze-frame activity to perform this.

2.3 Dramatic asides: sentence development

To take the previous activity further, use this to teach a convention of theatre: *the dramatic aside*. This is where an actor speaks their thoughts directly to the audience, unheard by the other characters on stage. Like their inner voice, it is often where Shakespearean characters reveal their true thoughts, which can be quite different to what they say in public. In Shakespeare's plays, the aside is often shown by the word (aside), italicised, in brackets at the start of the line. There are examples of this in *Macbeth, Romeo and Juliet* and other plays.

Based on the hearts and minds activity, give the children two paper sentence strips. On one, ask them to write a sentence spoken aloud to the other characters about their thoughts (the mind) about the plan to kill Caesar. On the other, they write a dramatic aside to deliver to the audience revealing their true thoughts (the heart). This can be a good point to teach about complex and compound sentences using conjunctions or punctuation.

Cassius might say:

> *Julius Caesar is a glorious hero of Rome, although I fear that he is becoming too powerful; yet when he is gone, maybe it will be time for me to take charge – wouldn't I look fine sitting on the throne?*

These are a lot of fun to perform aloud, especially when speaking deviously to the audience, so enjoy performing and discussing these as a class. This activity is good preparation for the short writing task, designing election manifesto posters.

2.4 More sinned against than Cinna: a class discussion about fairness

Curiously, there are two characters in this play called Cinna: Cinna the Conspirator, who appears in Act II, and Cinna the Poet, who appears briefly at the very end of the play. This play is hardly a factual documentary about the life and times of Julius Caesar where Shakespeare is duty-bound to give accurate names, so what is he up to here?

At the end of Act V, Cinna the Poet comes to a grizzly end at the hands of the mob when he is mistaken for the Cinna involved in the murder. This works on two levels. The first is how the death of an innocent man indicates that ancient Rome was often a brutal, chaotic and dangerous place, quite a contrast to the picture of orderly sophistication we often paint about the Romans. On the second level, Shakespeare is perhaps warning us about the need for order over anarchy.

In our experience, children have a strong opinion about the importance of following the rules and fairness! They should have plenty to contribute to a circle-time discussion about this. You might ask the children to think about the consequences of disorder. Ask them to suggest something that they don't enjoy doing at home: cleaning out the pet rabbit, tidying their bedroom, combing their hair, sharing with their sister. For one of these situations, what are the reasons for and against doing it? What are the consequences of not doing it, and how do these build up? It's an effective way to model using conjunctions (then, moreover, furthermore, ultimately, therefore) and to build up an argument or set of reasons – useful practice for writing the persuasive speeches later on in this unit of work.

> If I don't clean out the pet rabbit's hutch, then the hutch will start to smell. Furthermore, that might make the whole house smell of rabbit droppings. Moreover, the rabbit might get sick and have to go to the vets, which is very expensive. Consequently, mum and dad would have less money to spend on me. Therefore, it's best to keep the rabbit hutch clean even if I don't like doing it!

2.5 My best friend: freewriting task

For this task, discuss the idea of friendship by asking children to write about their best friend. This is an excellent link to the qualities for leadership explored in the **short and long writing tasks**. Ask the children to spend one to two minutes jotting down any words (adjectives, verbs, adverbs) or phrases (simile, metaphor) that relate to this idea. Pool them on the whiteboard, and then set the children to write for 10 minutes on this idea.

When finished, you do not need to ask the children to read their writing aloud. Instead, ask them to identify the most powerful sentence they have written, or the most unusual image they have created and write this down on a sentence strip for the working wall. The ideas should be drawn upon later in the unit of work.

3. Connection: cross-curricular links

History   The play is set in ancient Rome, and exploring the history of the period will help set the context for understanding the play. Looking at the part Julius Caesar and the Romans played in shaping Britain will also help make the story relatable to the children and where they live.

The Roman Empire and its impact on Britain (KS2)

KS2 objectives for this subject include:

- Julius Caesar's attempted invasion in 55–54 bc
- The Roman Empire by ad 42 and the power of its army
- Successful invasion by Claudius and conquest, including Hadrian's Wall
- British resistance, e.g. Boudica
- The Romanisation of Britain

RE   Roman religion

Alongside your scheme of work for RE, this would be an opportunity to learn about:

- Roman festivals and religious celebrations (e.g. the festival of Janus to celebrate the start of a new year)
- The differences between polytheism (e.g. Roman paganism, Hinduism) and monotheism (e.g. Christianity, Judaism and Islam)

PSHE   Voting and government

This play is about the transfer of power from a representative form of government to dictatorship and is an excellent opportunity to discuss key ideas about governance and key aspects of British values.

Alongside your scheme of work for PSHE, children might learn about:

- Different forms of government, including democracy
- Individual liberty and the right to vote
- Election procedures
- The rule of law

4. Illumination: responding through art

4.1 Trajan's column: depicting Julius Caesar in relief sculpture

For this activity, you will need sketchbooks, pencils, box cardboard or foam craft boards, scissors, glue, sponges, acrylic paint/stone-effect spray paint.

Perhaps one of the most incredible sights in ancient Rome (and in modern Rome too!) is Trajan's Column: a 30-metre-high commemorative monument erected in ad 113 by Emperor Trajan, dedicated to the memory of Julius Caesar (Figure 7.1). The column is covered by a **helical frieze** – a continuous frieze of scenes spiralling up the column – depicting Roman military might, their heroes and victories. Building your own Roman-style friezes out of layered cardboard would make a stunning art display and is an opportunity to tell a story visually.

Begin by looking at scenes from Trajan's column with the children. In their art sketchbooks, draw out images of figures from the scenes: a soldier in armour, a victorious image of Emperor Trajan, a Roman standard bearer or the god of the Danube river emerging from the water. Discuss the features of **relief sculpture**, and look to see how Emperor Trajan is himself depicted (he appears 58 times on the frieze!). Decide on a scene from the *Julius Caesar* story to depict in your frieze: the conspiracy in Brutus' orchard, the murder of Caesar, the speeches on the Senate steps. Make a plan of the scene on A4/A3 paper in landscape. Once the scene has been designed, the children are ready to start building their relief sculpture frieze. The key here is layers.

Start with an A4 piece of box cardboard or foam board as a background – the rest of the picture will be built on top of it. On another piece of box cardboard, draw the outline of the first character from their sketches, cut out and glue into place on the background. Cut out smaller pieces for the facial features, hair, armour, swords, clothes and so on, and glue them on, building up a 3D relief. Repeat for other characters and background scenes. To finish, sponge paint with white or grey acrylic paint, or spray with stone-effect spray paint. Leave to dry and display in sequence!

Figure 7.1 A detail from Trajan's Column in Rome.

Source: This file is licensed under the Creative Commons Attribution 2.0 Generic license. https://commons.wikimedia.org/wiki/File:Trajan%27s_Column_(II)_(7161067547).jpg

5. Application: writing

5.1 Short writing task – descriptive writing: election posters!

This story is about characters vying for power. Children might be familiar with prominent political election campaigns in Britain and the United States as well as school-based elections for school councillors or house captains. Central to any election campaign is a manifesto: a document that outlines the reasons why you should be elected. In this task, children will design a manifesto poster that outlines why they would be a better leader of Rome than Julius Caesar. This is a fun way to engage with the text but also deepens children's understanding of the main character.

Begin by discussing the reasons Caesar is the villain of this story both in terms of his actions and his personality flaws (this is called 'hubris'). Try to articulate these in dramatic, over-the-top language: *He is hungry for power; he is interested in his own glory; he throws his friends into the gutter; he won't listen to those who advise him.*

Then, ask the children to take this further to write contrasting statements about themselves. Looking at Brutus' and Mark Antony's speeches at the end of the play might help them inject some Shakespearean language into this writing.

> *Julius Caesar doesn't listen to his friend's advice, although I, sensitive Marek, would make sure I listen carefully to everyone. We are stronger together!*

Or something more ambitious . . .

> *Julius Caesar is a hungry and ambitious man with a wolf-like greed for power, whereas I, honest Fauzia, only have an appetite for the glory of all Romans!*

Aim for three or four strong contrasting sentences, and write them onto a poster alongside a photograph of the candidate (toga and wreath optional) with a winning smile. To finish, think of an election slogan for a title – e.g. "Popular Poppy wants your vote!" The posters could be printed or copied on aged paper and displayed around school.

5.2 Long writing task – Lend me your ears! Writing persuasive speeches

The drama, discussion and art activities explained in this chapter are designed to lead your class towards a written response to the play. As this play where oratory and persuasive language are key to the resolution of the plot, these writing activities focus on dramatic speeches inspired by the performances of Brutus and Mark Antony on the steps of the Roman Senate in front of the braying mob. These are intended to be written in pairs with a public performance at the end.

Read: To help prepare the children for this task, you will need to spend time performing and watching performances of the speeches. In print, both Leon Garfield's adaptation and the *Manga Shakespeare* version of *Julius Caesar* (2008) give an excellent overview of the speeches while still retaining the richness of the language. On film, the animated Shakespeare version of *Julius Caesar* demonstrates the speeches performed. From Hollywood, the powerful performances of James Mason (Brutus) and Marlon Brando (Mark Antony) in the 1953 black-and-white version of *Julius Caesar* show the speeches in a recreation of the scene on the steps of the Roman Senate. Draw children's attention to how they use persuasive language, and remind them of the election poster task. Ask the children to discuss which character they think is the most persuasive and why, finding evidence in the text or video to support their point.

From the text: Using photocopied versions of the script, cut out the part for Brutus and Mark Antony and arrange them as a continual text, using a page in the children's books for each character. Discuss the meaning of the words, and unpick some of the imagery such as Mark Antony's description of Brutus as "Caesar's angel" (Act III, Scene 2). Using highlighter pens, ask the children to identify one example of *how Caesar is described*, a word or phrase that shows *powerful emotion*, a *point of persuasion* and, for an extra challenge, an example of *figurative language*.

Extend the discussion to determine how the speeches are structured: an **eloquent introduction to the crowd** (e.g. *Friends, Romans, Countrymen, lend me your ears! I come to bury Caesar not to praise him*) + **what he did and why it happened** (e.g. *But, as [Caesar] was ambitious, I slew him.*) + **how he feels about it now** (e.g. *Now I shed tears for his love. It was not that I loved Caesar less, but that I loved Rome more.*) **= a paragraph of a speech**. As a class, use the annotations to write an example speech from each character. Do this on a large sheet of paper, and display on your working wall to refer to later.

Plan: First decide on the purpose for the writing. You could ask the children to rewrite the speeches for and against Caesar, or bring it up to date and ask them to write speeches explaining both sides of something relevant to their own lives: why homework is/is not a good idea, whether broccoli is/is not good for the soul, or whether bedtime should/should not be 8pm.

Working in pairs, decide whether you will be Brutus and argue against it, or Mark Antony and argue in favour. Look again at the structure of the speeches or the examples from the working wall, and make a quick bullet-point plan of the points each character will make. From these plans, model an example of these speeches and ask the children to write their own version.

Write: To extend, ask the children to write one or two further paragraphs for their speech supporting their argument. Focuses for writing are use of persuasive language to convince the audience, a clear structure to the speech and, where appropriate or for an extra challenge, use of Shakespeare's language. Develop further by including simple stage directions as cues for acting and body language as they perform.

So, if Brutus, in the modern day, was speaking up about his dislike for doing homework, it might look something like this:

Brutus: *Friends, Londoners, classmates, lend me your ears! 'Tis true that I have refused to do my maths homework this weekend. Hear me now and I shall explain.*

(sadly) As much as maths is important, my weekend is very short. As caring as my teacher is for setting the homework, I wish that she doth not have extra work by having to mark my homework.

And, yes, I now shed tears. (waving his fist in the air) But, classmates, it is not because I love maths any less: it is because I love watching the football on television more.

Children could work in pairs, with another writing in support or opposition to this speech. Although this is a challenging task, we have found that Year 4 children enjoy writing words to be spoken aloud. Composing a speech requires experimentation, so allow the children to work in draft before they try to compose in their exercise books.

Once written, allow the children to perform aloud for a small group with others giving feedback. Allow time to edit and redraft, perhaps with a focus on deepening the emotional language.

Share: The culmination of this project on *Julius Caesar* is a live performance of the speeches in front of an audience: the rest of the class, another group of children or, even better, their parents. For an authentic Shakespearean and Roman experience, you may allow this audience to heckle or be generally unruly (if you are feeling brave). To prepare for this, you may wish to revisit the drama activity "Friends and Romans" to focus on how body language and tone of voice can influence a live performance. Perform in a horseshoe with the stage at the front, and perform the speeches in pairs. You may wish to judge the most convincing of the speeches by volume of applause (although subsequent lynching and civil war are strictly optional).

Digital: Stop-motion animation is a perfect digital design project that challenges the children to collaborate and to make directorial decisions about staging a performance. For a stop-motion animation project, the children could work in small teams to depict one of the key scenes in *Julius Caesar*. The scenery can be built using Lego blocks and populated with Lego figures; children could use an edited version of the script and provide the voice-over themselves. Read more about stop-motion animation in Chapter 2.

Inclusive learning

To differentiate . . .

- As an alternative to the speeches, less-confident or EAL children might enjoy working together with a supporting adult to recreate the scene where Caesar is stabbed in the Senate.

- They could take part in a piece of collaborative writing where they write a short passage of dialogue for each conspirator and perform it as a group. This would be an excellent 'flashback' to perform at the beginning of the live performance.

Greater depth . . .

- For talented writers, greater depth can be encouraged by asking children to break away from the formulaic structure of the argument and experiment with a different approach. Ask them to independently research other famous speeches from more recent times: Martin Luther King Junior's "I have a dream," motivational speeches by Michelle Obama or Greta Thunberg's impassioned speeches on climate change.

Resources

Books to read as you teach

Appignanesi, R. (Abr.) (2008) *Julius Caesar: Manga Shakespeare*, London: Self Made Hero.
Garfield, L. (Abr.) (1992) *Julius Caesar: Shakespeare the Animated Tales*, London: Heinemann Young Books.
Garfield, L. (1994) *Shakespeare Stories II*, London: Victor Gollancz.
McCaughrean, G. (2017) *Stories from Shakespeare*, London: Orion.

Videos to watch as you teach

Julius Caesar (Shakespeare: The Animated Tales). (2013) [DVD] Directed by Yuri Kulakov. UK: Metrodome Distribution.
The Rise and Fall of Julia Caesar. (2018) [ONLINE] UK: ARTiculate Education Available at: www.articulateeducation.co.uk/p/gallery.html

8 Year 5, *Macbeth*

The play in one word: Greed

Macbeth – sometimes called "The Scottish Play" by superstitious actors – is one of Shakespeare's most famous tragedies. It tells the story of legendary soldier and nobleman Macbeth, whose life and fate is transformed following a chance meeting with three witches on a barren heath after a battle. The witches awaken his greedy ambitions, leading him to murder and the slow unravelling of both his mental health and political authority.

Macbeth is deliciously gruesome and plays on some of Shakespeare's most famous themes: power, corruption, greed and betrayal. Ideas of prophecy, regicide and consequences build on the themes of other plays such as *Julius Caesar*.

Studying this play with Year 5 offers a wealth of stimulating opportunities for collaborative and creative responses to the story through art, drama, music and creative writing.

Background to *Macbeth*

Theatre was certainly a place where Shakespeare provoked his audiences to think about religion and politics of the day. When *Macbeth* was performed for King James I in 1606, both the king and the audience would have recognised the pressing political themes: anxiety about treason, fear of a chaotic royal succession, the fractious relationship between England and Scotland, and the dangers of witchcraft.

The idea for the plot of *Macbeth* is likely to have come from Raphael Holinshed's historical account (albeit one written long after the fact) in his book *Chronicles of Scotland* (1587). In Holinshed's version, Macbeth and Banquo acted together to kill the Scottish king. But as King James believed himself a direct descendant of Banquo, Shakespeare wisely played safe and rewrote Banquo as a noble, innocent victim.

Witchcraft was taken very seriously in early modern England – a preoccupation of the king and his people – and this would have been accepted as fact rather than fantasy. Seeing this depicted on stage would have entranced and revulsed audiences just as the characters bewitched Macbeth. As King of Scotland (where he was known as James IV), James had felt the need to instigate the North Berwick Witch Trials (1590–1592) after a violent storm preventing his sailing to Denmark was attributed to a possible witches' curse.

Quite rightly, King James lived in fear of conspiracy and treason. The Gunpowder Plot, a failed attempt to assassinate the king by blowing up the Houses of Parliament in 1605,

DOI: 10.4324/9781003023944-11

happened the year before *Macbeth* was performed. The plot of Guido Fawkes and others would have caused a sensation in Shakespeare's time and was probably a source of inspiration for Macbeth's plot against Duncan. Shakespeare's depiction of a treasonous nobleman who gets what was coming to him would have intrigued and satisfied him.

Macbeth *in five minutes: a summary of the play*

Macbeth

Bang a stick on the floor three times and begin. All hail Macbeth!

Be not afraid, gentle people. That thunderous noise is just a storm after battle, that ghostly mist a common experience in this part of Scotland. ⇒ **Illustration 4.1**. But behold! Two figures emerge from the mist: it is Macbeth and Banquo leaving the field of combat, victorious. The day has been long and bloody, fighting the enemies of their beloved King Duncan. Victory is sweet, and the two warriors and life-long friends anticipate a night of celebration.

Eerie, hypnotic voices cut through the swirl of fog and clashes of thunder: fair is foul and foul is fair, Hover through the fog and filthy air. Three hideous witches emerge from the gloom, halting Macbeth and Banquo in their tracks and enchanting them with their words. All hail, Macbeth, who will be Thane of Cawdor and, one day, king. And to Banquo, they tease: All hail you, who will not be king but happier as your children will one day be kings. Spooked and terrified, the warriors return to meet with King Duncan, where they are greeted warmly as heroes of Scotland. ⇒ **Inspiration 1.1**.

Macbeth is indeed rewarded and just as the witches predicted, he becomes a great chieftain: thane of Cawdor. But rest not, gentle people, the witches have enchanted Macbeth; this noble warrior harbours dark, greedy ambition and greed quickly spirals out of control. ⇒ **Incubation 2.4**.

Prepare yourselves for more shocking deeds. . . . Thrice woe. With Lady Macbeth at his side, he doth murder King Duncan. Is this a dagger I see before me? He doth murder Banquo who suspects him of this terrible deed. He doth murder all of brave MacDuff's family; MacDuff a loyal lord, also suspicious of Macbeth's deeds, who now vows revenge for his family. ⇒ **Incubation 2.3**.

But guilt haunts them.

Banquo's ghost doth torment him. That canst not say I did it, gasps Macbeth. ⇒ **Incubation 2.1 and 2.2**.

The blood they have spilt doth torment Lady Macbeth. Out damn spot. What, will these hands ne'er be clean? Gentle people, such is her anguish, she ends her own life.

As Macbeth hurtles into madness and despair, he learns from the witches a most strange idea – he should fear MacDuff but no man born of woman can harm him. Is he invincible? ⇒ **Application 5.1 (Short writing task)**. Armed with a cloak of immortality, he returns to his castle at Dunsinane, where a battle is looming. Canst thou hear the drums of war?

Duncan's family and MacDuff march to seek their revenge on greedy, murderous Macbeth. As Macbeth faces MacDuff in combat, he taunts him. . . . I bear a charmed life. But MacDuff's reply chills his blood – Turn, hellhound, turn! ⇒ **Inspiration 1.2**. Macduff was from his mother's womb untimely ripped. Macduff reveals he has not been born; he has been taken out of his mother by an operation.

Doomed, Macbeth fights. Lay on, Macduff! They duel fiercely; with a sweeping sword stroke, Macduff strikes Macbeth's head from his very body. Thud! ⇒ **Application 5.2 (Long writing task)**.

And so it ends, this dreadful tale of greed, darkness and death, the end of a man called Macbeth.

Famous quotations

Out damned spot, out I say!
Lady Macbeth hallucinates Duncan's blood on her hands (Act V, Scene 1)
Yet I will try the last! Before my body I throw my warlike shield: lay on, Macduff!
In despair, Macbeth vows to fight on against Macduff (Act V, Scene 8)
Double, double toil and trouble!
The three witches chant as they carry out their schemes (Act IV, Scene 1)

Did you know?

- Although we don't learn Lady Macbeth's name, the wife of historical Macbeth was named 'Gruoch' or 'Gruach'.
- If you say 'Macbeth' in a theatre, you are meant to walk three times in a circle anti-clockwise, then either spit or say a rude word. The play is thought to be unlucky due to the goriness of it all.
- **And a joke for you** … Who is the greatest chicken killer in Shakespeare? Macbeth, because, to be fair, he did murder most foul.

Teaching *Macbeth*

Summary

These activities incorporate role play, discussion, dance and art to bring a class topic on *Macbeth* to life. The activities have been designed to lead your class towards a dramatic re-enactment of the final battle between Macbeth and Macduff. There are also jumping off points for science, DT and maths.

If you have less time, you should focus on re-enacting the scene with the witches (Inspiration 1.1) and the hip-hop spells in iambic pentameter (Application 5.1, short writing task).

1. Inspiration: starting with a flourish

1.1 Speak if you can! Dramatic improvisation

The play begins on the battlefield with Macbeth and Banquo meeting the three witches, or weird sisters, withered and wild. Exploring this scene with music, speech and sound effects is the perfect way to set the scene for this play. Record this so you can listen again or share with parents.

Seat the children in a horseshoe with the performance space at the front. Give several children drums, and ask them to beat a slow and steady rhythm as the class perform. Begin with a call and response, the teacher reading the lines and the children replying. *When shall we three meet again?* And continue until: *Fair is foul and foul is fair*. Ask the children to stand and repeat the chant, but this time experimenting with different voices (whispering, cackling, shrieking), body percussion (stamping of feet, clapping hands) and sound effects (wind, lightning, rain). To extend, provide the lines on paper and ask the children to break into groups of three to four to practise the scene. Once each group has practised, these can be performed for the class, possibly as a musical round.

Then it is time to bring in the actors. Still in a circle, split the children into three groups: Macbeth, Banquo and the witches. Using an abridged version of the script, read the lines of Banquo and Macbeth as a call and response. You could invite two children to step into the circle while this is bring performed – quite intimidating! Follow with the witches speaking the three lines of temptation for Macbeth (All hail, Macbeth, hail to thee, Thane of Glamis!)

While the sound effects and percussion continue, ask the children to step into the circle and improvise their own temptations for Macbeth and Banquo using the formula, "All hail, Macbeth, hail to thee, you will be the most famous man in the whole world!" "All hail, Banquo, hail to thee, all of these riches can be yours!" To extend this, you could use the **decision alley** drama technique (see Chapter 3) to shower Macbeth and Banquo with temptations.

This activity not only sets the mood of the play but also helps the children find their voices and practise key lines from the play. It is likely to be noisy and lively, but we have found that building that kind of atmosphere usually helps the children (and staff) to lose themselves in the experience!

1.2 Turn hell hound! A speaking game

This deception game can include the whole class, and, again, this is a good way to get the children talking with a performance voice and memorise some of the key lines from the play. Choose one player to be on – call them 'Macbeth' – who faces away from the rest of the children. In a circle or at desks, the remaining pupils close their eyes. The teacher selects three pupils to be the secret witches by tapping them on the shoulder; they will provide the mystery voices. In turn, they say the same sentence in a disguised voice. Choose a line from the play, e.g. *When shall we three meet again? In thunder, lightning or in rain?* After each turn, ask Macbeth to turn around using Macduff's command "Turn, hell hound!" and guess who the mystery voices were. This is a fun game for warm-up or wind-down that builds their knowledge of the play.

2. Incubation: embedding themes and ideas

2.1 Rise and fall: plotting the story as a graph

This activity will help the children develop an understanding of the whole story and trace Macbeth's emotional journey through the story. You may wish to do this as you read a version of the story to the children or as you watch a video of the story such as *The Animated Tales* version.

Using a graphic version of the story, such as *Mr Shakespeare's Plays* or Gareth Hinds' graphic novel *Macbeth*, ask the children to use a tablet or camera to photograph five or six key pictures that show turning points for Macbeth. Discuss why the children have chosen these images and how they summarise the story.

Give the children a blank line graph with a blank *x* and *y* axis. The *y* axis can show the height of his nobility or the depths of his treachery; the *x* axis shows his journey through the story. On the blank graph, plot the highs and lows of the six key moments the children chose earlier. Discuss what this graph represents and how it helps you understand Macbeth's emotional journey as well as his political one. Is there one moment in the story when Macbeth crosses a line of no return, or could he always be saved?

2.2 The crimes of Macbeth: a discussion activity

Once the children have been introduced to the main points of the story, they are ready to explore the character of Macbeth. Start with this chin-scratcher: *can killing ever be justified?* Killing the enemies of King Duncan in battle made Macbeth a hero and a legend in Scotland. Killing Duncan, however, made Macbeth a murderer. How are these events different? Give pupils the opportunity to think on each case separately before making their cases in discussion (Figure 8.1).

Introduce a set of incident cards listing Macbeth's crimes, e.g. murdering the king, ordering the death of Banquo (his best friend), killing soldiers in battle, taking part in witchcraft. In pairs, ask the children to arrange the crimes in order from most justified to least justified. Ask the groups to justify their choices, especially any grey areas. Start to build up a case against Macbeth by dividing the incident cards into two clear categories: justified – unjustified. No sitting on the fence! This activity is good preparation for a role play activity for putting Macbeth on trial (Inspiration 2.3).

To take this one step further, you can also ask the children to write on sticky notes how Macbeth would answer each of the charges. For example:

Crime Killing King Duncan.	**Reason** Duncan was an old man and Scotland needs a young, energetic king like me. I am sorry for what I did but I was thinking of the good of the country.

Can children give convincing reasons for Macbeth's crimes?

We have found that children really enjoy putting forward their view. Sometimes these debates can become suitably fierce, so it's always a good idea to give pupils strategies for demonstrating healthy but polite disagreement ("I see your point but . . . "). This kind of activity often reveals to the children that Macbeth is not a monster but a nuanced, almost sympathetic, character. It is exactly why this play is a tragedy!

Figure 8.1 Actor Bob Frazer as Macbeth. Discussing the severity of Macbeth's crimes with children deepens their understanding of this complex character.

Source: This file is licensed under the Creative Commons Attribution 2.0 Generic license. https://commons.wikimedia.org/wiki/File:Bob_Frazer_(Macbeth)_in_Macbeth_at_Bard_on_the_Beach._Photo,_David_Blue.jpg

2.3 Putting Macbeth on trial: a plot-building drama game

To follow on from the discussion task, you are now ready to engage in some lively role play by putting Macbeth on trial for his crimes. To prepare for this activity, exploring and debating Macbeth's crimes (Inspiration 2.2) will help give them some of the most pressing crimes committed by Macbeth but also his counter claims.

First, discuss the main crimes of Macbeth and make a list – vote on which of three are your main charges. Seat the children in the round with a stage at the front. Select a judge to ask the questions, and ask the children to play the jury – they will vote on how convinced they are by Macbeth's answers. To give the children an idea of how to play the character, consider modelling the role yourself and trying to explain yourself fully:

> *Your honour, ladies and gentlemen of the jury, I admit that I did meet the most foul witches that morning on the heath and I did hear their words, but I was not one of them. I was an innocent victim who fell to their witchcraft. I beg you! They are responsible, not noble Macbeth!*

Scottish accent is optional. You may wish to draft in new Macbeths to take your place as you demonstrate. At the end, ask the jury to vote on whether or not Macbeth is guilty (he always is!), but do suggest that they can change the ending of the story if they wish and acquit him if the argument is convincing.

Then split into groups of four or five to replay the scene again with one child as Macbeth, one as the judge and the others as the jury. Rotate before performing in front of the class.

This activity can be expanded to include other characters – Macduff, Banquo and Lady Macbeth – as witnesses, although the children will need to have an understanding of how these characters fit into the tale.

2.4 Graffiti character posters: vocabulary development

Many actors have played Macbeth on stage and screen. As we discussed in Chapter 2, the 'gappiness' of Shakespeare's stage direction means that different actors play the role in different ways. Allowing the children to find the version of the character they find most convincing draws their attention to stagecraft.

Look at a selection of photographs of actors playing Macbeth on the stage. Some notable ones include Peter Woodward (1991), Mark Rylance (1995), Pete Postlethwaite (1995), Ray Fearon (2016) and Masachika Ichimura (2017). Looking at each image, think about which part of the story is being depicted, what words describe this 'Macbeth' or what you imagine him saying at that moment. On sticky notes, you could ask the children to start building vocabulary for each picture: adjectives (wild, furious, thoughtful), powerful verbs (pleading, raging, plotting) or figurative language (a man possessed, a wild dog, a puppet on a string). Use extracts of the text you are using to glean Shakespearean words to describe him: bloody, bold, serpent.

On top of the photographs, add descriptive words using graffiti pens. Words can be overlaid, shaped or stylised, with the cursive style changed to match the feeling behind the word (e.g. jagged lines for furious, small letters for weak or innocent). Over the body of Macbeth, you might write a line of his dialogue that he might be speaking at this point in the story, again gleaned from the text or written by the children. This makes an effective word bank as well as a striking piece of artwork.

This activity may also be extended to depictions of other prominent characters from the story such as Lady Macbeth (Kate Fleetwood, Tara Fitzgerald), Banquo (Canada Lee, Paddy Considine) and the witches in productions by Barry Kyle (1983), Robin Lough (2018) and in Umabatha/Zulu Macbeth (1997).

2.5 The abandoned castle: freewriting task

For this task, show the children a picture of a ruined castle (for example, Slains Castle in Scotland) and ask them to imagine walking up to the castle in the dark! Talk with the children about why the castle might be abandoned and what it would be like to be there. This will help embed the setting of the story and help capture the mood for the writing tasks and the artwork later in this unit. Ask the children to spend one to two minutes jotting down any sensory vocabulary, including a range of word classes (adjectives, verbs, adverbs) or figurative language (simile, metaphor) that relates to the castle. Pool them on the whiteboard, and then set the children to write for 10 minutes on this idea.

When finished, you do not need to ask the children to read their writing aloud. Instead, ask them to identify the most powerful sentence they have written, or the most unusual image they have created, and write this down on a sentence strip for the working wall. The ideas should be drawn upon later in the unit of work.

3. Connection: cross-curricular links

Science   Mixing magical potions using strange and exotic components plays a significant and influential role in Macbeth, driving the narrative to its dramatic conclusion. The play offers an opportunity to experiment with more earthly substances in a study of properties and changes of materials.

Year 5 science objectives (materials) include:

- Compare and group together everyday materials on the basis of their properties
- Know that some materials will dissolve in liquid to form a solution, and to describe how to recover substance from a solution
- Demonstrate that dissolving, mixing and changes of state are reversible changes

PE (dance)   The sword fights between characters and the wild movements of the witches as their stir their cauldron could be represented through dance.

Year 5 PE objectives include:

- Perform dances using a range of movement patterns

Design Technology/Maths   The Iron Age hill fort at Dunsinane in Scotland is thought to be Macbeth's castle, the site of his fateful final battle. Opportunities arise for addressing STEM activities through designing stronger structures to help Macbeth defend his crown. Free comprehensive resources and presentations for this activity can be found on the website of the Institution of Engineering and Technology, www.theiet.org/education

The KS2 objectives for Design Technology and Maths include:

- Understanding how different shaped structures perform under load
- Understanding how structures can be strengthened and reinforced

4. Illumination: responding through art

4.1 So fair and foul a day: gloomy watercolour landscapes

For this activity, you will need inspiring landscape images, pencils, charcoal, sketchbooks, watercolour paints, thick art paper.

Michael Foreman's illustrations in Leon Garfield's *Shakespeare Stories* are fantastic and an excellent starting point for creepy, ominous artwork. Most impressive is the image of three witches appearing in the sky above Macbeth.

To explore this with the children, begin by looking at the landscape paintings of Georgia O'Keeffe (*Lake Georgia*, 1922), Chinese landscape painter T'ang Yin 唐伯虎 (*Dreaming of Immortality in a Thatched Cottage*, C.16) or Scottish artists Shona Barr, Carina Prigmore and Kirstie Cohen (www.kilmorackgallery.co.uk). Draw the children's attention to how the artists use colour to express mood or create atmosphere; how scenes are composed with big skies and hills dwarfing small buildings and people to emphasise loneliness; how features such as trees and forests, buildings and people are drawn. Allow the children to get the feel for this genre by sketching these images in pencil or charcoal.

In sketchbooks, create an atmospheric colour chart using watercolour paints. Recreate the shades in some of the example images as well as other cool colours, and ask the children to give the colours suitably gloomy names: *spectral grey, phantom yellow, enchanted blue*.

To bring this together, get the children to create gloomy watercolour images inspired by the landscape of *Macbeth*. Use watery paints on thick paper to roughly depict the land, sky and lakes. Landscape features such as the witches' heath, a ruined castle, a forest, ravens in the sky or witches around the cauldron can be added using different shades of pencil. As well as making an interesting display, these can later be used as backgrounds for *Scratch* animations.

5. Application: writing

5.1 Short writing task – double trouble: writing hip-hop witches' spells

British rapper Akala has shown that Shakespeare's verse has many similarities with hip-hop music (see *The Hip-hop Shakespeare Project*, www.hiphopshakespeare.com), especially the use of **iambic pentameter** (the de-DUM, de-DUM rhythm). Helping children to see that Shakespeare, like many of today's musicians, was first and foremost a poet and an entertainer rather than a 'writer' may help them to make a stronger connection with his work. With this in mind, use this as an opportunity to write raps based on the chants of the three witches.

To prepare, the children will need to know the overview of the story and watch Akala rapping Shakespeare's poem, *Sonnet 18* at TEDxAlderburgh in 2016.

Return to the text and read the song of the witches which begins with the famous lines "Double, double toil and trouble; fire burn and cauldron bubble." Count the lines of the poem and how they rhyme (14 lines, seven pairs of rhyming couplets). You can also look at the use of poetic techniques such as **alliteration** (baboon's blood) and vivid, vibrant **imagery**.

Read the lines through several times: first by talking them, then by chanting them to a clapped beat. Changing the delivery of the lines to suit the rhythm is a step away from reading and one towards performing.

To turn this into a rap like Akala's, the children will need to change the poem to fit the **pentameter** – that is 10 syllables in each line. They can do this by modifying or rewording the original lines. As a class, look at the first two couplets and try to change them so they have 10 syllables in each line, perhaps like this:

> *Double, double toil and trouble;*   ⇒   *Double, double, toil, toil, double troubles;*
> *Fire burn and cauldron bubble.*   ⇒   *Fire is burning and the cauldron bubbles.*

In small groups, ask the children to look at another pair of couplets. Discuss the words and what they mean, then experiment with changing the lines to fit the 10-syllable structure. Again, focus on alliteration to add in adjectives. So "fillet of a fenny snake" can become: "Fat fillet of a furry fenny snake" and so on. Allow the children to practise performing the lines to different instrumental hip-hop tracks before coming together to perform together.

To develop this into a longer poem, ask the children to collaborate in groups to write 14 lines of their own featuring strange ingredients for the witches' potion. They could decide on what the incantation is for (to banish homework? To create a magic cocktail giving amazing strength?). This is an ideal open-ended writing task that promotes creative use of language within a clear structure, collaboration and inclusion. Working as a group will also give them confidence to perform together. When they have finished composing their poems, perform to music as a class.

5.2 Long writing task – lay on Macduff! Writing playscripts for the final battle

This task will draw on the drama and discussion activities from earlier in this project, notably the crimes and trial of Macbeth. Scripting an exchange between the two main characters of the play will be an opportunity to showcase the children's understanding of the characters, the plot and of performance and drama techniques.

The key scene for this is the final battle between Macbeth and Macduff beginning with Macduff's line "That way the noise is" until Macbeth's death (spoilers!). Even in the original play, this scene is quite brief – the audience already knows why they are enemies. From text and screen versions, you will notice that the scenes are almost devoid of dialogue, and this is your opening for creative writing. You might want to show how this compares to the fight sequence between Darth Vader and Obi Wan Kenobi from *Star Wars, Episode IV: A New Hope* (1977) to show how a sword fight, interspersed with dialogue, can be a powerful spectacle.

> **Read:** Provide the children with an abridged copy of the script for Macbeth and Macduff's final showdown. Read the scene in pairs, taking a turn as each character and discuss the language as a class. It is important to draw the children's attention to Macbeth's reaction to Macduff's challenge in the face of the obvious truth: his own death. Is his "I will try the last!" evidence that really Macbeth is noble and worthy of redemption? Could this scene end differently with Macduff forgiving Macbeth?
>
> You may want to show a video version of this scene to illustrate it clearly such as the excellent (and gore-free) *Animated Tales* version. Note how the dialogue in the script they have compares to what is recited on screen - it is heavily reduced, and just

the bare bones are left. Point out to the children that their writing challenge will be to fill these gaps with their own dialogue.

From the text: Children look at the exchange in the abridged version. They will see unusual words verb forms such as *hast* and *losest*, as well as unusual phrases such as "my soul is too much charged" and "accursed be". Begin by asking the children to 'translate' the argument between Macbeth and Macduff into their own way of speaking. How would it sound in the playground?

To play with this scene, ask the children to imagine a situation where the characters may be arguing over something from their everyday experience – Macduff has stolen Macbeth's pencil, Lady Macbeth telling Macbeth to wash his hands, the witches discussing the weekend's football results – and writing it in 'Shakespearean' English (see the guide to Shakespearean grammar in Chapter 2). The children we have taught have enjoyed the freedom to experiment in this way, and it has given them much more confidence in reading Shakespearean scripts.

Plan: Now the children are ready to plan the exchange between Macbeth and Macduff. Remind the children of the crimes of Macbeth activity and the trial (Activities 2.1 and 2.2). On a double page in their exercise books, use one side to choose three accusations that Macduff might put to Macbeth, e.g. he murdered his family, he killed King Duncan, he became involved in witchcraft. Then make notes about how Macbeth might answer these charges (three for each charge), justifying his actions. Would he apologise? Has he realised his mistake? Will he try to blame someone else? Once completed, turn these into short paragraphs. Read these drafts aloud and discuss them – how could they be developed to reveal more of Macbeth's character? You might also discuss how Macduff would approach this: would he save his most powerful argument until last, or would it come bursting out straight away?

Once they have planned the structure of the dialogue, return to the script. In pairs, ask them to decide where the conversation they are planning will fit in. Once they have found the right place, they can decide what of the original text they will keep for their scripts to serve as an introduction. Using highlighter pens, pick out the bare bones of Shakespeare's text to retain.

Write: To make the most of what the children have learned on this topic, draw up a list of criteria for what they would like to include in this writing: Shakespearean insults and greetings (see Chapter 3), descriptive language from the poster activity (**Incubation 2.3**) or other words or expressions picked out from the texts they have read.

Using this, model an example exchange between the characters. It might look like this:

Macduff: *Lo! Hear me now, thou errant, burley-boned horn-beast! Thou art guilty, foul Macbeth, of a most terrible crime. Murdered good King Duncan in his bed, thou did'st! Thou art a cowardly, hasty-witted measle. What sayest thou?*
Macbeth: *Hie! How darest thou! I am thy king, thou loggerheaded, elf-skinned footlicker! A good sir, noble Duncan was, and one did not desire to murder him. But that gent was old. A young, energetic king, Scotland did need.*

Discuss the structure of this dialogue and how it might be changed or developed. Then, in pairs, the children can collaborate to write a script of two to four dialogues. Read and talk about how they are effective. Remember, in most of Shakespeare's plays we only know about the characters by what they say. How well does what the children have written capture the feelings of both characters?

Once written, discuss how the scene will end. Will Macduff kill Macbeth? Or will the tyrant king repent and be allowed to live? Edit and redraft as appropriate.

Share: These exchanges are perfect for a live performance and could be paired with dance routines developed in PE lessons (see Connection). To condense these into a short and powerful live performance for the whole class, ask the children to select their favourite exchange from their writing to perform followed by some brief sword duelling. A whole series of Macbeths and Macduffs could perform their lines in turn before asking the audience to vote on whether Macbeth should be killed or spared, before performing a final death/redemption scene. You might discuss how the characters could be dressed to help the audience keep up with who is who (all Macbeths wear a crown, all Macduffs wear white, for example). It would be an excellent way to showcase this unit of work.

Digital: Children could use the *Scratch* animation platform to respond to the story. This might include an animated game where items are dropped into the witches' cauldron. Each item that is dropped could trigger a recorded line from the Spell Raps writing task. Similarly, the children might animate the fight scenes between Macbeth and Macduff with their paintings as backgrounds for the action. They could record their lines of dialogue as a voice-over.

Inclusive learning

To differentiate . . .

*   For EAL or lower reading abilities, consider simplifying the text, but take care to retain some of the original richness of the language. The Witches' Rap could be written and performed as a group along with a dance routine written by the children.

Greater depth . . .

*   Pupils can be challenged to rewrite scenes in a contemporary setting. The witches could be three children planning mischief at home or at school. Fight scenes could be relocated to squabbles in the playground, an episode of their favourite soap opera or even a spat over Twitter or text. Visualising and modernising texts can help children recognise the relevance of Shakespeare's writing in the modern day.
*   Descriptions of events could be written from different viewpoints such as that of Banquo or Lady Macbeth.

Resources

Books to read as you teach

Garfield, L. (1985) *Shakespeare Stories*, London: Victor Golanz.
Garfield, L. (Abr.) (1992) *Macbeth: Shakespeare the Animated Tales*, London: Heinemann Young Books.

Hinds, G. (2015) *Macbeth (Shakespeare Classics Graphic Novels)*, Somerville, MA: Candlewick Press.
Rosen, M. (2016) *What's So Special about Shakespeare?*, London: Walker Books.
Williams, M. (2008) *Mr William Shakespeare's Plays*, London: Walker Books.

Videos to watch as you teach

Macbeth. (2013) [DVD] (Shakespeare: The Animated Tales). UK: Metrodome Distribution.
Macbeth. (2014) [ONLINE] UK: Shakespeare's Globe [Viewed 1 January 2021] Available at: www.shakespearesglobe.com/learn/playground/animation-videos/#macbeth
Macbeth Explained by Author Michael Rosen. (2016) [ONLINE] UK: BBC Newsround [Viewed 1 January 2021]. Available at: www.bbc.co.uk/newsround/36099745
The Throne of Blood: Trailer. (1957) [ONLINE] [Viewed 1 October 2020] Available at: https://youtu.be/LY7ETlO1KB8

9 Year 6, *The Winter's Tale*

The play in one word: Change

The Winter's Tale has often been presented as a 'problem' play. The tragic opening scenes veer wildly towards the comic half-way through; the character of 'Time' is used to conveniently pass 16 years; the conclusion is hasty with its *Dallas*-style ending. These things have been pointed at to suggest that this was Shakespeare past his peak. And yet, the story still presents a moving and dramatic emotional journey for the characters and for the audience.

The play touches on themes of jealousy, fortune and extreme actions, and it has universal appeal that you will find in many myths and legends, fairy tales and dramas and soap operas today. For Perdita, the baby who was lost, the story is about her being found and also finding herself. This is a story about change. Indeed, this makes the play ideal for the end of Key Stage 2.

Year 6 is a transition year with all the highs and lows that it entails – mixed emotions, changes, leaving old friends and finding new ones. So, *The Winter's Tale* is the perfect play for young pupils fast growing up and ready to face new adventures.

Background to *The Winter's Tale*

Shakespeare is not thought to have travelled, and apart from some fanciful theories that he served as a soldier in Italy, there is no evidence that he ever left England. Yet, most of his plays are set around the Mediterranean, which represented exoticism, high culture and escapism in the minds of his audiences.

Shakespeare took his inspiration for *The Winter's Tale* from Robert Greene's romantic story *Pandosto*, which tells the story of the king of Bohemia who wrongly believes that his wife is pregnant by his old friend, the king of Sicily. (Robert Greene was an author and a contemporary of Shakespeare. He is now best remembered for insulting Shakespeare as an "upstart crow", too big for his boots!)

Shakespeare, however, inverts the locations, opening his play in Sicily rather than in Bohemia as Greene does. Although one explanation is that Sicily was notorious for crimes of jealousy and revenge whereas Bohemia was a land known for romance, it is more likely to have been a safer, political choice on behalf of Shakespeare. When the play was written, around 1609-1611, Rudolf King of Bohemia was an ally of his fellow Protestant monarch King James I of England. With Sicily under the rule of Catholic Spain, a rival of England, casting the king of Sicily as the villain was a good way for Shakespeare to please his king – a man who was the main sponsor of his theatre company.

DOI: 10.4324/9781003023944-12

The Winter's Tale *in five minutes: a summary of the play*

The Winter's Tale

Bang a stick on the floor three times and begin.

⇒ **Inspiration 1.1 and 1.2**. Ladies and gentlefolk, I present to you a story of opposites: of love and suspicion, of kindness and cruelty, of winter and summer. Verily, they say a sad tale is best for winter, and, aye, this tale has much sorrow in it.

I introduce to thee the ruler of Sicily, King Leontes. In his fair home on the Mediterranean Sea, under warm skies, he entertains his oldest friend, King Polixenes of Bohemia. Leontes' wife, Hermione, is expecting a new child. Truly, suspicion can make people act in the strangest of ways, and Leontes has grown to believe that the child has been fathered by Polixenes. Fearing for his life, Polixenes flees back to Bohemia.

But what blockish, apish stuff is this? Hermione is a loving, faithful wife; Polixenes a loyal and trusted friend. How swiftly jealousy infects a suspicious mind, and Leontes throws his wife into prison, where she gives birth to a little girl. Cruelly, Leontes orders his friend Antigonus to abandon the baby in a distant, remote and wild place. Stricken with grief, Hermione dies. . . . Or does she?

Whither shall Antigonus go, dear gentlefolk? To Bohemia of course, the kingdom of Polixenes if you recall. Here, he abandons the baby, whom he calls Perdita - the lost one - to her fate. Suddenly, Antigonus is attacked by a wild bear, who chases and eats him clothes and all. Fortunately, Perdita is spared such a grizzly end, and her crying attracts a shepherd who lives close by and rescues her. ⇒ **Incubation 2.1 and 2.3**. A kind and loving man, the shepherd raises her with his family as if she was his own child. Perdita's life is simple but happy; she is oblivious to her wealth and privilege as a princess and is loved by everyone in the village. ⇒ **Incubation 2.2**.

Tick. Tock.

Time passes, and 16 years flash by. But the past is not forgotten, and Perdita's life is about to change again. Meet Prince Florizel, son of Polixenes. Florizel decides to amuse himself at the summer festival, where he disguises himself as a shepherd, and here, he meets the lovely Perdita. O, knotted brains! Perdita is really a princess living as a shepherd girl; Florizel is really a prince disguised as a shepherd boy. Confounded and confused? This truly is a most tangled web. But, as they dance most merrily and revel at the festivities, the two fall in love, neither knowing their true identities. Florizel vows to marry her. Such fury hath the king! Royalty must marry royalty. Little doth he know of Perdita's true self! Florizel and Perdita hatch a most hasty plan to escape and marry in a land far away. Whither will they go? To Sicily, of course, the home of King Leontes, where this story began all those years ago.

Tick. Tock.

For 16 long years hath Leontes mourned his foolish actions. O, woe! On greeting Prince Florizel and Perdita, he hath no idea that this fair young woman is in fact his own flesh and blood, until King Polixenes arrives from Bohemia. Such news he doth bring! The baby abandoned on his shores 16 years ago is Perdita, Leontes' lost daughter! There is much happiness, and friendships are mended. ⇒ **Application 5.1 (Short writing task)**. But sadness lingers as Hermione, long dead, cannot share in this joyous moment.

In his grief, King Leontes had honoured his most beloved wife with a statue which they all visit to pay their respects. Astonishingly, the statue of Hermione comes to life. A miracle! Did she really pass out of life? Or has she been in hiding and grieving for her long-lost family?

This tale of change, of love and suspicion, of kindness and cruelty, of winter and summer is over, and everyone, apart from poor Antigonus - eaten by a bear - lives happily ever after. ⇒ **Illumination 4.1; Application 5.2 (Long writing task)**.

Famous quotations

A sad tale's best for winter.
Queen Hermione's son, Mamillius, on his favourite type of story (Act II, Scene 1)
This is the chase. I am gone forever.
Antigonus's last line as he is chased from the stage by a bear . . . (Act III, Scene 3)
Exit, pursued by a bear.
. . . and the stage direction that proves it! (Act III, Scene 3)

Did you know?

- Antigonus, Perdita, Florizel and others travel by boat to the shores of the land of Bohemia. In fact, Bohemia is in modern-day Czechia and completely landlocked!
- Appropriately, the name Perdita means 'lost' in Latin.
- Some have speculated that Shakespeare may have used a real bear on stage to chase off Antigonus as there was a bear-baiting arena next to the Globe Theatre. It seems more likely that it was a person in a bear suit!

Teaching *The Winter's Tale*

Summary

Incorporating role play, discussion and art, and with links to PSHE, science and design technology, these activities will help you explore the emotional journey of *The Winter's Tale* and its themes of loss and discovery, friendship and consequences. Exploring the key scene of the abandonment and discovery of the baby Perdita, these activities will support designing maps, making silent films and writing a newspaper report reflecting on the events.

If you have less time, focus on incubation activities (2.1, 2.2 and 2.3) where the baby Perdita is lost and found before writing the recipe for a friend (Application 5.1, short writing task).

1. Inspiration: starting with a flourish

1.1 Tangled web: a circle time activity

The Winter's Tale has a complex plot. Characters are lost and found, intentions are misread, identities are changed. It is a story of transition: of place, of time, of season and of feelings - a real soap opera storyline that the writers of *EastEnders* would be proud of. Before you read the story to the children, play a game to show how tangled and confused our emotions can be, especially when facing change.

Sit in a circle with a large ball of wool in the centre. One person holds on to the loose end of the wool. Ask pupils to think of something nice to say about someone in the group or something that person might be good at. As they do, throw the ball of wool to that person. They hold onto the ball of wool and throw it to someone else as they say something positive about that person. After ensuring everyone has had a turn, look how tangled the wool has become, criss-crossing through the circle. Reflect on how pupils felt, both being a giver and a receiver of positive comments.

Once the children are confident with the idea (and if you think your class will respond well to it) explore other feelings: anger, embarrassment and jealousy. Ask the children to discuss one of the challenges or disappointments that they have felt at school before throwing the ball of string to *someone who has helped them through it*. What you will end up with is a complex web of feelings and emotions that has built over time between the cast of characters – your class! It's an ideal metaphor for both this story and their transition to their next school.

1.2 A mystery basket: discussion

One of the main plot points of *The Winter's Tale* is when the shepherd discovers the child Perdita in a basket on the shore after she has been sent away from Sicily. Pique the children's curiosity before reading them the story.

Seating the children in the round, place a basket in the middle with a toy baby or doll inside, covered with a large blanket. Set the scene: This box was left in the classroom this morning, and you have no idea what is inside. There was a note with it that said if you uncover this basket, you are responsible for what is inside. A real dilemma!

First, ask the children to discuss in pairs what they think is inside. Then a bit of logical thinking. Should they remove the blanket? What would the consequences be? Make a note of the key arguments for and against before deciding what to do – these phrases and arguments will be useful for the drama activities that will follow. In our experience, children won't be able to resist knowing what is underneath, and expect some surprise and shock when your class realise they are now responsible for a baby! You might tuck in the pages of the story along with the baby, either from this resource, or from a language-rich version adaptation. Read the story.

2. Incubation: embedding themes and ideas

2.1 Baby dilemma: drama

When the kindly shepherd finds Perdita on the Bohemian shore, he faces a dilemma. Should he find who the baby belongs to? Should he leave it? Should he take it home with him? For the shepherd, the choice is not a hard one – he takes the child home to a loving household – but would the children feel the same?

Building on the mystery basket discussion, ask the children to stage the **decision alley** drama activity (see Chapter 3). Place the basket at the far end, and ask a child to role play the shepherd. As the shepherd walks towards the baby, ask both sides of the 'alley' to whisper his inner thoughts. If the side urging him to leave the baby are more convincing, the shepherd can walk closer to where he started. This will make those arguing for him to rescue the child up their game a little!

When the character has made their choice, **hot seat** the shepherd and investigate why he has made his decision. You might then reveal to the children that a bag of gold and royal documents were also found next to Perdita's basket, which of course the old shepherd took (although he can't read the document to know she was a princess). Does this change the children's opinion of him now? What might he use the money for?

Children can break out into small groups to play the hot-seating activity, perhaps finishing by giving the shepherd the choice of sticking with his decision or changing it. Some of this might get a little gossipy and lively, but go with it. This is how Shakespeare's audiences would have interacted with the events on the stage. Here you might ask the children which other stories they know that feature a baby lost and found. It is a popular theme: Moses in the Bible, Mowgli from *The Jungle Book*, Paris in the *Iliad*, even Luke Skywalker in *Star Wars* are 'lost' babies. What do the children foresee being the problems as Perdita grows older?

2.2 Lost and found: character development of Perdita

Although this is not explored in the play, it seems reasonable that the shepherd and his wife might have tried to look for Perdita's parents or at least enquire if anyone in the village had recently lost a baby! This is an opportunity to consider both the character of Perdita and of the shepherd family that takes her in – both of which will be useful for the long writing task.

The shepherd and his son discover the baby at the start of Act III, Scene 3: "Mercy on 's, a barne a very pretty barne! A boy or a child, I wonder? A pretty one; a very pretty one." There is very little in this scene to describe Perdita, but there is enough to give the impression she is a pretty, good-natured baby. Some creative licence can be taken from there. Establish here what the characters (not the audience!) **know for certain** about the baby (found on the beach, a bad storm, a shipwreck, called Perdita, found with some money), **what they might know** (might have come from the ship, might have been an unwanted child – the shepherd speculates euphemistically that the baby might be the result of some "behind door work") and **what they might want to know** (where she came from, if she is royalty, what they should do etc.). We have found children enjoy this kind of speculation on a story, proposing possibilities and exploring the 'gappiness' of Shakespeare.

Use these ideas to create 'found' posters for the baby. These can include some details of the discovery, some of the speculation and what anyone claiming her should do. Keep these brief and concise as the aim here is to flesh out the characters and deepen understanding of the plot, although you can challenge your children to use Shakespearean language: *barne* for baby is one example. Display around school.

2.3 Silent movie: drama and filmmaking

Build on the poster activity by exploring the discovery of Perdita in more detail. Begin by acting out the scene at the start of Act III Scene 3 using an abridged script. Seat the children in the round and run through the scene once without pausing to explain the meaning of the words. Repeat with a fresh cast, although this time focus on how the shepherd's words reveal his character and motivation. Finally, repeat the scene again but without any words at all – just actions, body language and facial expressions to respond to the dialogue.

Delivering the story without dialogue was a challenge for directors of the silent movie era, who often chose to direct classic stories such as Shakespeare's plays. Show to the children a silent version of *The Winter's Tale* from 1913 directed by Baldassare Negroni (available for free at https://player.bfi.org.uk/free). As they watch, ask them to focus on how facial expression and body language stand in for the dialogue – it is quite exaggerated! *Why is this? How do camera shots such as close-up of the face help emphasise meaning? Would audiences at least have got the gist of the story from this? What differences are there between this version of the story and that of the original play?*

Pause the video just before the scene where Perdita is abandoned (around 25 minutes). In groups of four or five, ask the children to recreate the next scene: from Antigonus' arrival in Bohemia with the baby, the leaving of the baby, Antigonus' fate and then the discovery by the shepherd. Ask the children to role play the scene silently, and record with video cameras. These productions can be as lavish or as simple as you have time for. Use free editing software to piece the clips together. As an extra challenge, you may ask children to create intertitles to describe the action and to move the narrative along. There are several examples on-line. Add suitable music to convey an appropriate mood to the video. Watch, share and discuss.

2.4 Being lost: freewriting task

For this task, ask the children to remember a time they were lost. Almost every child will have experienced this, just as Perdita does in the story, so this task will help children empathise with the main character and also see how Shakespeare played on themes most of us can relate to. In addition to where and when, discuss the heightened emotions of feeling lost. A small child might feel that they are suddenly alone in the world, when in reality their mum and dad are just in the next aisle of the supermarket. Ask the children to spend one to two minutes jotting down emotional vocabulary (adjectives, verbs, adverbs), adverbials and figurative expressions (simile, metaphor) that relate to feeling lost. Pool them on the whiteboard, and then set the children to write for 10 minutes on this idea.

When finished, you do not need to ask the children to read their writing aloud. Instead, ask them to identify the most powerful sentence they have written, or the most unusual image they have created, and write this down on a sentence strip for the working wall. The ideas should be drawn upon later in the unit of work.

3. Connection: cross-curricular links

This play would be ideal to link to your school's transition materials for the children leaving primary school and moving on to secondary education. The character of the passing of time, the idea of moving to a new place as Perdita did and learning about growth and change are all relevant.

PSHE/RSE   Teachers could also use their school's PSHE programme lessons to discuss issues that relate to this story – for example: communities, stereotypes, prejudices, aspirations and relationships.

The Department for Education guidance on relationships education (2020) states that children should learn about:

- **Respectful relationships mindful of difference** ⇒ Perdita is a migrant living with an adopted family. Consider the challenges she might face being transplanted to a new country.
- **Being safe and establishing boundaries** ⇒ discuss consent and the treatment of women in this story.
- **PSHE – Transition** Explore the theme of change further by preparing for the transition to KS3. There are many resources free available online covering this significant milestone in children's lives, e.g. www.youngminds.org.uk, www.third spacelearning.com, www.twinkl.co.uk.

Geography   This play is all about contrasting locations, so use this to link to a geographical comparison between where the children live and a contrasting location, geographical skills and fieldwork, or perhaps an investigation to show how Shakespeare's representation of Sicily and Bohemia is incorrect.

The KS2 objectives for geography include:

- use maps, atlases, globes and digital/computer mapping to locate countries and describe features studied
- use the eight points of a compass, four and six-figure grid references, map symbols and key to build their knowledge of the United Kingdom and the wider world
- understand geographical similarities and differences through the study of human and physical geography

Science   The passing of time and changes are integral to the telling of *The Winter's Tale*. Explore the huge themes of Evolution and Inheritance, and discover the inspirational Mary Anning, Charles Darwin and Alfred Wallace.

Year 6 objectives for Science (Evolution and Inheritance) include:

- recognising that living things have changed over time and that fossils provide information about living things that inhabited the Earth millions of years ago
- identifying how animals and plants are adapted to suit their environment in different ways and that adaptation may lead to evolution

4. Illumination: responding through art

4.1 Painting inspired by Jean-Noël Vandaele

For this activity, you will need images by Vandaele, sketchbooks, paper, pencils, oil pastels, poster paints, acrylics, marker pens, corrugated boards, cameras.

Contemporary Flemish artist Jean-Noîl Vandaele is well-known for his "Drawing Shakespeare" series, featuring bright, blocky depictions of scenes from Shakespeare's plays. With simplified backgrounds and bold, featureless characters, his images use colour and shape to evoke feeling similar to Matisse's paper-cut collages and paintings in the Tingatinga tradition. The artist has yet to draw a picture from *The Winter's Tale*, so this is the perfect opportunity to work with your children to fill in that gap!

Begin by looking at examples of Vandaele's paintings from plays the children will know well (*Romeo and Juliet* and *Macbeth*) as well as the portrait of Shakespeare himself. In sketch books, annotate copies of the pictures with notes about colour, shape and style. Allow children to cut out and collate parts of the pictures – figures, trees, buildings all feature – before sketching their own versions in pencil. The way Vandaele draws hands and mouths are particularly interesting. Experiment with oil pastels and poster paints to apply colour.

There are lots of vivid scenes in the play – e.g. the pursuit by the bear – so allow children to choose which they would like to focus on. Children could sketch from memory, but more effective is to use posed freeze-frame photographs with their classmates. Posing and arranging the characters is an important lesson in aesthetics and directorship. To encourage blocky, simplified drawings in Vandaele's style, consider letting children draw with marker pen on A3 corrugated plastic boards. Unnecessary lines can be removed and mistakes corrected before colour is applied with unmixed acrylic paint. Border lines can be added using marker pens.

These bright images would make a striking display arranged alongside key quotations from the play. You could even share it with the artist via Twitter @jnvandaele.

5. Application: writing

5.1 Short writing task – instructional writing: a recipe for a friend

In *The Winter's Tale*, Perdita is a princess, living as a shepherd's daughter. When she meets and falls in love with Florizel, his father King Polixenes is furious because he does not want his son to marry someone below his status. This raises powerful questions about judging people before you know them that can be explored through writing. With new friendships on the horizon in secondary school, this is certainly an issue to discuss and reflect upon.

Embed these ideas by creating a recipe for the perfect friendship. Begin by discussing what qualities the children look for in a friend. Take this further by discussing how a new friendship can help them in different situations and how the 'ingredients' of one friend might complement those in another. Make lists of ideas and ask the children to identify which are the most important to them and why.

To write this as an instructional text, you will need to revisit the features of this genre perhaps by reading examples of recipes: imperative verbs (stir, mix, fold, fry etc.), adverbs (gently, carefully, brisky), technical language (150g of wisdom, one heaped teaspoon of kindness) and the structure of this text-type (numbered lists, bullet points).

Model for the children an example line from the friendship recipe that shows the ingredient and why it is important:

1   First, add 150g of trust and 150g of loyalty to a large person-shaped bowl. Mix thoroughly so they are perfectly combined.
2   Add two free-range jokes and whisk until they laugh so hard their shells crack up.

Invite the children to share their ideas, and build up the recipe as a class before directing children to write their own. These collected 'recipes' would make a wonderful addition to a transition book for the children, and a school friendship cookbook (The Great British Friendship Bake-Off, perhaps?) would be a valuable learning tool for younger children.

5.2 Long writing task – writing a newspaper report

This task will draw on many of the drama and discussion activities from this unit of work. Children will also need a broad overview of the whole story to weave those details into the writing.

This long writing task will involve the children writing about the life of Perdita. For this outline, we have looked at a newspaper report that focuses on the discovery of Perdita by the shepherd. Depending on the interests of the children, they could look at another scene (e.g. her miraculous discovery) or another character (e.g. the miraculous revival of Hermione) or present the story in another format such as a blogpost or a magazine feature.

> **Read:** For this activity, revisit the features of a newspaper report. To tell the story of Perdita's amazing discovery, begin by looking at real examples recounting the dramatic return of lost children. There are lots of examples about long-lost family being reunited online.
>
> As they read the text, draw their attention to the structure of a newspaper: the layout, how key information is conveyed (the *who, where, when, what, why* and *how* of a news story), and examples of emotive language. Looking at a range of newspapers and discussing the purpose of news reports – to inform but entertain – will also prepare children for writing. Pick out some of the sensational language used in newspapers to hook their readers in: *shocked, bombshell, stunned into silence, rocked.*
>
> Comparing the same story told in different formats – for example, a newspaper v. online – will also draw the children's attention to how this writing is put together.
>
> **From the text:** Provide the children with a summary of the text from Act III, Scenes 1 to 3, where Antigonus has left Sicily with baby Perdita. The children will have already performed this scene earlier in this topic, so remind them by watching their silent films again.

In pairs, look at a paper copy of the script. This could be presented as an incident report of the abandoning of the baby. If someone read this script without knowledge of the rest of the story, how would they interpret the events? As they read, ask the children to annotate the script to identify answers to the journalistic questions. For example, for 'Who?', children can circle the names of characters and note down in very simple sentences what each character did in this scene. Focus on actions and precise details.

(Who?) Antigonus: He stepped out of his rowing boat carrying a wicker basket. The man walked on the beach and placed the basket carefully on a sand dune. A large black bear appeared and chased him towards the forest. He was not seen again.

If there is not clear evidence from the text, then children can infer what might have happened and perhaps indicate this in a different colour.

(When?) The events happened early that morning, just before sunrise: the shepherd was making his rounds.

Identify key quotes, Shakespearean words; perhaps surmise where other characters were at this time (King Leontes was inspecting troops at his castle in Sicily; Queen Hermione was assumed dead).

To take this activity further, the children could role play the scene again with one child acting as a TV news reporter sent to interview the characters. Other characters who don't feature here could be interviewed for their comment. This kind of activity embeds what the children know about a story and challenges them to make inferences and use deduction to fill in the gaps.

Plan: Once children are familiar with the structure of a news report and the key points of the story, create a paragraph-by-paragraph writing plan that will help them tell their version of events. Using the structure of the example texts will help the children see how to reveal the information about the events of Perdita's mysterious discovery a bit at a time.

The children will need to consider:

- The purpose and audience of a newspaper report.
- A standout headline (which they may write last as happens in real life).
- The story summary in 10 words or less.
- A short opening paragraph that tells the whole story in one or two sentences.
- A series of short paragraphs that answer the journalistic questions of who, what, where, when, why, who said what . . .
- Key quotes from characters who feature: from the text, what did the shepherd say when he found her?

Write: Keep the opening paragraph short. In pairs, ask the children to explain the 'bare bones' of the key moment for their story to each other in one minute. Then ask them to do it again, but in 30 seconds. Show them how difficult it is to get across key information very quickly. Once they have got it down to around three or four sentences, ask them to write it out on paper sentence strips or on a whiteboard. Challenge the children to use scissors or a board rubber to remove all the unnecessary words from their explanation until they have it down to just two or three sentences.

Model how to develop their annotated incident report and writing plan into a series of short paragraphs. Again, the focus here should be the sensational use of language to convey the facts:

> The shepherd was stunned to find a small basket sitting there on the ground. He was even more flabbergasted to see that it contained a poor, defenceless barne. The infant is said to be in a healthy condition.

They will need to see examples of how to drop in Shakespearean language lifted from the text, which may be done via reaction quotes from an eyewitness:

> A local villager has also expressed her concern for the child: "Forsooth, who would leave a fair child out in the wild like that? Do they not know that bears, most savage and grizzly, roam these woods? An absolute disgrace, it is!"

If the children are writing a version of the story for an online newspaper, challenge them to include features of online texts in their writing: tweets, hashtags, links to other stories and even online adverts for bear repellent!

To edit, revisit the criteria for writing an effective piece of journalistic writing. Help the children identify two or three areas of their writing that might be improved, noting that this is how a sub-editor would recommend changes to a real journalist. Allow time for redrafting.

Share: Once the children have completed their reports, have fun sharing them around the school. Copies could be left in school registers for teachers to read to their classes; snippets of the writing could be included on the school newsletter or put up on pretend sandwich boards outside the school. This might be the catalyst for encouraging children to contribute to a school newspaper with reports written in the same style.

Digital: The digital platform *Twine* allows users to design branching narratives, or 'choose your own adventure' stories (see Chapter 2). As *The Winter's Tale* is full of chance happenings and fortuitous events, *Twine* is ideal for getting children to imagine alternative endings and possible plot lines.

Drawing the plot of the story out as a branching story map (see Figure 9.1) is a good place to start. There's no need to plan the whole story, but having the first few steps will get them started. Beginning with the abandonment of Perdita, ask the children to simplify the plot from this point into five or six key moments. This will form the spine of the story. However, starting with the first event, imagine a parallel universe where she is not found by the shepherd but by someone else. The bear returns? Or a wolf, perhaps? Now we have two pathways through the story. At each further stage, imagine two more possible outcomes. In some, Perdita might come to a grizzly end, closing off that pathway, but in others, her story might continue to grow in unexpected

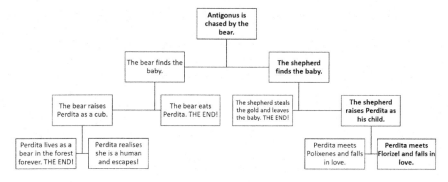

Figure 9.1 A branching narrative for retelling *The Winter's Tale* in *Twine*.

ways. Once the story is mapped out, children can write a few descriptive sentences to explain the action to the readers. Children will be amazed at how quickly the story builds up. When finished, the stories can be posted online, and other children can 'play' them as interactive storybooks.

Inclusive learning

To differentiate . . .

- Children who are less confident with acting can take on other roles such as recording or photographing the action.
- Children who struggle with writing might instead write their news story as a 'piece to camera' TV report. Start with the drama, record them speaking, and use that as a basis for the first draft of a script. This could be done collaboratively in a pair.
- Dyslexic readers might be provided with a script pre-annotated with alternatives for unfamiliar words.

Greater depth . . .

- As an extra challenge, more confident writers could include complementary texts to include with their article, e.g. a weather report, a health and safety warning for coming into contact with a bear, a diary extract expressing Hermione's sadness and bewilderment at being imprisoned. Learning to shape and enhance a text may provide evidence of deep understanding and mastery of writing.

Resources

Books to read as you teach

Garfield, L. (Ed.) (1994) *The Winter's Tale (Animated Tales)*, London: Heinemann Young Books.
Garfield, L. (1994) *Shakespeare Stories II*, London: Victor Gollancz.

Williams, M. (2008) *Mr William Shakespeare's Plays*, London: Walker Books.
The Winter's Tale (A Shakespeare Children's Story) (2012), Leicester: Sweet Cherry Publishing.

Videos to watch as you teach

Racconto D'inverno (The Winter's Tale). (Italy, 1913) [ONLINE] Directed by Baldassare Negroni, Italy [Viewed 1 May 2020] Available at: BFi Player.
The Winter's Tale (Shakespeare: The Animated Tales). (2013) [DVD] Directed by Stanislav Sokolov. UK: Metrodome Distribution.

Appendix

National Curriculum objectives

Year 1: *The Tempest*

Activity	Subject area	Objective
1.1	**English: spoken language**	• participate in discussions, presentations, performances, role play/improvisations and debates
1.2	**Art and design**	• to use a range of materials creatively to design and make products
	English: reading	• participate in discussion about what is read to them, taking turns and listening to what others say
2.1	**English: writing**	• Year 1 vocabulary, grammar and punctuation objectives • Sequencing sentences to form short narratives
2.2	**English: spoken language**	• participate in discussions, presentations, performances, role play/improvisations and debates
	English: reading	• discussing word meanings, linking new meanings to those already known
2.3	**Design Technology**	• select from and use a wide range of materials and components, including construction materials, textiles and ingredients, according to their characteristics
3	**Connection – see Chapter 4 for objectives**	
4.1	**Art and design**	• to use a range of materials creatively to design and make products • to use drawing, painting and sculpture to develop and share their ideas, experiences and imagination about the work of a range of artists, craft makers and designers
5.1/5.2	**English/reading**	• becoming very familiar with key stories, fairy stories and traditional tales, retelling them and considering their particular characteristics • making inferences on the basis of what is being said and done
	English: writing	• Year 1 vocabulary, grammar and punctuation objectives • Sequencing sentences to form short narratives • Evaluating their writing with the teacher and other pupils, proofreading to check for errors in spelling, grammar and punctuation
	Computing	• Use technology purposefully to create, organise, store, manipulate and retrieve digital content

Year 2: *A Midsummer Night's Dream*

Activity	Subject area	Objective
1.1	**English: reading**	• discussing the sequence of events in books and how items of information are related • becoming increasingly familiar with and retelling a wider range of stories, fairy stories and traditional tales
1.2	**Music**	• use their voices expressively and creatively by singing songs and speaking chants and rhymes • play tuned and untuned instruments musically
	English: reading	• participate in discussion about books, poems and other works that are read to them and those that they can read for themselves, taking turns and listening to what others say
2.1	**English: writing** **Art and design**	• writing down ideas and/or key words, including new vocabulary • to use a range of materials creatively to design and make products
2.2	**English: writing**	• Year 2 vocabulary, grammar and punctuation objectives • expanded noun phrases to describe and specify
2.3	**English: spoken language**	• participate in discussions, presentations, performances, role play/improvisations and debates • articulate and justify answers, arguments and opinions
	English: writing	• planning or saying out loud what they are going to write about
2.4	**English: reading (non-statutory)**	• Role play and other drama techniques can help pupils to identify with and explore characters. In these ways, they extend their understanding of what they read and have opportunities to try out the language they have listened to.
3	**Connection - see Chapter 5 for objectives**	
4.1/4.2	**Art and design**	• to use a range of materials creatively to design and make products • to develop a wide range of art and design techniques in using colour, pattern, texture, line, shape, form and space
5.1/5.2	**English/reading**	• discussing their favourite words and phrases • drawing on what they already know or on background information and vocabulary provided by the teacher • predicting what might happen on the basis of what has been read so far
	English: writing	• Year 2 vocabulary, grammar and punctuation objectives • writing for different purposes • proofreading to check for errors in spelling, grammar and punctuation (for example, ends of sentences punctuated correctly)
	Computing	• use technology purposefully to create, organise, store, manipulate and retrieve digital content

Year 3: *Romeo and Juliet*

Activity	Subject area	Objective
1.1	**English: spoken language**	• speak audibly and fluently with an increasing command of Standard English • participate in discussions, presentations, performances, role play/improvisations and debates
1.2	**English: spoken language**	• use relevant strategies to build their vocabulary
	English: writing	• in narratives, describing settings, characters and atmosphere and integrating dialogue to convey character and advance the action
2.1	**English: spoken language**	• speak audibly and fluently with an increasing command of Standard English • participate in discussions, presentations, performances, role play/improvisations and debates
	English: writing	• Lower Key Stage 2 vocabulary, grammar and punctuation objectives • discussing and recording ideas
2.2	**English: reading**	• listening to and discussing a wide range of fiction, poetry, plays, non-fiction and reference books or textbooks • checking that the text makes sense to them, discussing their understanding, and explaining the meaning of words in context
2.3	**English: writing**	• participate in discussion about both books that are read to them and those they can read for themselves, taking turns and listening to what others say
	Computing	• use technology purposefully to create, organise, store, manipulate and retrieve digital content
2.4	**English: writing**	• composing and rehearsing sentences orally (including dialogue), progressively building a varied and rich vocabulary and an increasing range of sentence structures • organising paragraphs around a theme
3	**Connection – see Chapter 6 for objectives**	
4.1	**Art and design**	• to create sketch books to record their observations and use them to review and revisit ideas • to improve their mastery of art and design techniques, including drawing, painting and sculpture with a range of materials
5.1/5.2	**English: reading**	• increasing their familiarity with a wide range of books, including fairy stories, myths and legends, and retelling some of these orally • preparing poems and play scripts to read aloud and to perform, showing understanding through intonation, tone, volume and action discussing words and phrases that capture the reader's interest and imagination • recognising some different forms of poetry (for example, free verse, narrative poetry)
	English: writing	• Lower Key Stage 2 vocabulary, grammar and punctuation objectives • in narratives, creating settings, characters and plot • proposing changes to grammar and vocabulary to improve consistency, including the accurate use of pronouns in sentences

Year 4: *Julius Caesar*

Activity	Subject Area	Objective
1.1	**English: spoken language**	• maintain attention and participate actively in collaborative conversations, staying on topic and initiating and responding to comments
1.2	**English: spoken language**	• articulate and justify answers, arguments and opinions
2.1	**English: reading**	• draw inferences such as inferring characters' feelings, thoughts and motives from their actions and justifying inferences with evidence
	English: spoken language	• consider and evaluate different viewpoints, attending to and building on the contributions of others
2.2	**English: reading**	• draw inferences such as inferring characters' feelings, thoughts and motives from their actions and justifying inferences with evidence
	English: writing	• Lower Key Stage 2 vocabulary, grammar and punctuation objectives
		• in narratives, creating settings, characters and plot
2.3	**English: writing**	• compose and rehearse sentences orally, progressively building a varied and rich vocabulary and an increasing range of sentence structures
2.4	**English: reading**	• identifying main ideas drawn from more than 1 paragraph and summarising these
		• identifying how language, structure, and presentation contribute to meaning
2.5	**English: writing**	• composing and rehearsing sentences orally (including dialogue), progressively building a varied and rich vocabulary and an increasing range of sentence structures
		• organising paragraphs around a theme
3	**Connection – see Chapter 7 for objectives**	
4.1	**Art and design**	• Improve their mastery of art and design techniques, including drawing, painting and sculpture with a range of materials
5.1/5.2	**English: reading**	• increasing their familiarity with a wide range of books, including fairy stories, myths and legends, and retelling some of these orally
		• preparing poems and play scripts to read aloud and to perform, showing understanding through intonation, tone, volume and action discussing words and phrases that capture the reader's interest and imagination
		• identifying themes and conventions in a wide range of books
	English: writing	• Lower Key Stage 2 vocabulary, grammar and punctuation objectives
		• in narratives, creating settings, characters and plot
		• organising paragraphs around a theme
		• proposing changes to grammar and vocabulary to improve consistency, including the accurate use of pronouns in sentences
	Computing	• select, use and combine a variety of software that accomplish given goals

Year 5: *Macbeth*

Activity	Subject Area	Objective
1.1	**English: spoken language**	• select and use appropriate registers for effective communication
	Music	• play and perform in solo and ensemble contexts, using their voices and playing musical instruments with increasing accuracy, fluency, control and expression
1.2	**English: reading**	• learning a wider range of poetry by heart
2.1	**English: reading**	• drawing inferences such as inferring characters' feelings, thoughts and motives from their actions, and justifying inferences with evidence
	English: writing	• use further organisational and presentational devices to structure text and to guide the reader
	Computing	• select, use and combine a variety of software that accomplish given goals
2.2	**English: spoken language**	• develop understanding through speculating, hypothesising, imagining and exploring ideas
2.3	**English: spoken language**	• participate in discussions, presentations, performances, role play/improvisations and debates
2.4	**English: writing**	• selecting appropriate grammar and vocabulary, understanding how such choices can change and enhance meaning
2.5	**English: writing**	• Upper Key Stage 2 vocabulary, grammar and punctuation objectives • noting and developing initial ideas, drawing on reading and research where necessary
3	**Connection – see Chapter 8 for objectives**	
4.1	**Art and design**	• improve their mastery of art techniques with a range of materials • to create sketch books to record their observations and use them to review and revisit ideas
5.1/5.2	**English: reading**	• preparing poems and plays to read aloud and to perform, showing understanding through intonation, tone and volume so that the meaning is clear to an audience • drawing inferences such as inferring characters' feelings, thoughts and motives from their actions, and justifying inferences with evidence • predicting what might happen from details stated and implied
	English: writing	• Upper Key Stage 2 vocabulary, grammar and punctuation objectives • in narratives, describing settings, characters and atmosphere and integrating dialogue to convey character and advance the action • assessing the effectiveness of their own and others' writing • perform their own compositions, using appropriate intonation, volume, and movement so that meaning is clear
	Computing	• select, use and combine a variety of software that accomplish given goals

Year 6: *The Winter's Tale*

Activity	Subject Area	Objective
1.1	**English: spoken language**	• give well-structured descriptions, explanations and narratives for different purposes, including for expressing feelings
1.2	**English: spoken language**	• participate in discussions, presentations, performances, role play/improvisations and debates
	English: reading	• asking questions to improve their understanding • drawing inferences such as inferring characters' feelings, thoughts and motives from their actions, and justifying inferences with evidence
2.1	**English: spoken language**	• give well-structured descriptions, explanations and narratives for different purposes, including for expressing feelings
2.2	**English: writing**	• use further organisational and presentational devices to structure text and to guide the reader
2.3	**English: reading**	• predicting what might happen from details stated and implied • asking questions to improve their understanding
2.4	**English: writing**	• Upper Key Stage 2 vocabulary, grammar and punctuation objectives • noting and developing initial ideas, drawing on reading and research where necessary
3	**Connection - see Chapter 9 for objectives**	
4.1	**Art**	• to create sketch books to record their observations and use them to review and revisit ideas • to improve their mastery of art and design techniques, including drawing, painting and sculpture with a range of materials • about great artists, architects and designers in history
5.1/5/2	**English: reading**	• increasing their familiarity with a wide range of books, including myths, legends and traditional stories, modern fiction, fiction from our literary heritage, and books from other cultures and traditions • drawing inferences such as inferring characters' feelings, thoughts and motives from their actions, and justifying inferences with evidence • explain and discuss their understanding of what they have read, including through formal presentations and debates, maintaining a focus on the topic and using notes where necessary
	English: writing	• Upper Key Stage 2 vocabulary, grammar and punctuation objectives • identifying the audience for and purpose of the writing, selecting the appropriate form and using other similar writing as models for their own • using a wide range of devices to build cohesion within and across paragraphs • evaluate and edit by proposing changes to vocabulary, grammar and punctuation to enhance effects and clarify meaning
	Computing	• design, write and debug programs that accomplish specific goals, including controlling or simulating physical systems; solve problems by decomposing them into smaller parts

Index